$AVVY WOMEN $MART CHOICES:

42 $MART CHOICES WOMEN CAN MAKE IN FINANCIAL AND ESTATE PLANNING

MARCIA VANDERWOUDE & DENISE MCGREGOR

$avvy Women, $mart Choices:
42 $mart Choices Women Can Make in Financial and Estate Planning

© 2005 Marcia VanderWoude
MLV Consulting Group, LLC
West Olive, Michigan

ISBN: 0-9764402-0-2

Library of Congress Control Number: 2005905838

Printed in the United States of America
05 06 07 08 09 // 10 9 8 7 6 5 4 3 2 1

DEDICATION

This book is dedicated to my God and the two wonderful children He gave me, Sara and Michael.

Marcia VanderWoude

ENDORSEMENTS

"Marcia VanderWoude and Denise McGregor have written a book that I have known needed to be written for many years. Statistically, 80% of American women will experience widowhood and 50% will experience divorce. For those reasons alone women need to be prepared to handle their financial matters wisely. This book, using personal stories, communicates in an incredibly effective way the unique challenges and opportunities that women have when it comes to managing the wealth that has been entrusted to them. Whether that wealth is a great amount or a small amount, smart choices are essential for long-term financial security. I am delighted that this book has been written and hope it becomes a bestseller."

Ron Blue, President, *Christian Financial Professionals Network*

"*$avvy Women, $mart Choices* provides practical life lessons for anyone who wants to be financially successful but unsure as to where to start. By relating individual experiences, Marcia VanderWoude and Denise McGregor illustrate how women can achieve financial independence through education and perseverance. The advice offered is applicable for novice investors as well as the sophisticated investor. Anyone looking for solid, foundational guidance should consider reading this book."

Michelle VanDyke, President/CEO, *Fifth Third Bank, West Michigan*

"This breakthrough book shows each woman how to achieve and maintain her own financial independence— faster than she may have thought possible!"

Brian Tracy, Author, *Getting Rich Your Own Way*

"I really enjoyed reading the case method approach to solving investment problems. The real life experiences make, what could be dry subjects, come alive and vivid. I imagine readers will find this book rewarding, interesting and touching.

Donald Yacktman, President, *Yacktman Asset Management Company and Yacktman Funds, Inc.*

ACKNOWLEDGEMENTS

I am so grateful to my pastors Andy DeJong and Bill Rigg in their immense contribution to my spiritual journey, as well as their encouragement and prayers.

My co-author Denise McGregor is a wonderful writer whose perfectionism saved me from haste. Eva Bliss, my copy editor, was masterful in punctuation and other items long forgotten since college English. Josh Visser, graphic designer, gave face and shape to these stories.

I am thankful beyond words to all the women who shared their stories and smart choices.

Paula and Jane Vanderleest, in their hard work on the first draft and continuing interest in the final product, gave me the boost I needed to keep going.

Chic Bain, my long-time friend and client has encouraged me the whole way and is designing my web site. Tamara Lubic turned a fresh eye to the manuscript when my patience was flagging.

My close "sisters" who grace my life with friendship include: Susan Anderson, Joy Brande, Ruth Ann Brown, Nancy Bryant, Jan Durr, Jeanne Duthler, Judy Gezon, Carolyn James, Evonne Kok, Adele Krhovsky, Jill Maitzen, Cele Mereness, Pam Moeke, Barb Nigro, Joyce Oostdyk, Sally Ransford, Marilyn Rottschafer, Jean Rybock, Ann Scarff, Jani Sepanik, Kathy Smith, Rainie Smith, Margaret Spelman, Jan Walhout, and Kris Weidenaar.

For their skill I thank the Veltman Retirement Specialists who so carefully and wisely advise my clients in their financial planning.

Other contributors were Daryl Vogel, Michael Toth, and Henry Evenhouse, C.P.A., with factual data.

The support and encouragement of my sweet husband Ken Weidenaar has been invaluable.

CONTENTS

Part Three: Advanced Strategies

Part Four: The Starter Guide to $mart Choices

INTRODUCTION

THE CHOICE TO BE A SAVVY INVESTOR

While working as a broker in the financial industry for more than twenty years, I met many women who had left all money decisions to the men in their lives—their fathers, sons, husbands, and even their ex-husbands. It wasn't long before I realized that these women were putting themselves in financial jeopardy. How could they be sure that their men were making smart choices? Should they assume these men would always be in their lives to handle their financial matters? Could they trust these men to do the best for them? Did they care about or even understand the financial principles upon which these men were making joint investments on their behalf?

My misgivings about how women were handling—or neglecting—their money led me to become passionate about working with them and educating them in investment strategies. It also reconfirmed a core belief that all women could be savvy investors if they chose.

It sounds simple enough, but why wouldn't women choose to make smart choices? Some are stuck in the Miss Scarlett syndrome and tell themselves that they won't think about it today...they'll think about it tomorrow. They might even say to themselves, "When my husband dies, I'll figure it out." Then the husband dies, and they are lost. Many just aren't interested in investing or having anything to do with finances. Others use their spending as an emotional crutch and not wanting to feel deprived, refuse to take responsibility for managing their money. Still others are amply provided for in their relationships, but they haven't a clue as to what things truly cost. Feeling entitled to a steady stream of money, they are absolutely panicked if a sudden life change, such as divorce, forces them to survive on a budget.

By refusing to step up to the plate and care for their own net worth, women are easy prey for anyone who wants to relieve them of their money. If this seems a little harsh, read Victoria's story "A Tragedy of Trust" and see how a very successful career woman was set for retirement. She deferred her investment decisions to a broker who was more interested in putting her into speculative investments than watching over her principal. When her portfolio had dwindled to a mere fraction of its former value, she was given the excuse of a "declining market" and the broker refused to return her calls. Her only recourse was a lengthy, complex arbitration process that has required her to hire her own attorney and wait two years before she could schedule an arbitration hearing. Instead of retiring early, she has been forced to work longer.

I have seen so many women hand over ownership of their money to less competent hands with comments like "whatever you think is best," and then turn a blind eye to that person abusing their funds and their lives. This has prompted me to refer women investors to women financial advisers who, in my opinion, tend to be relationship-oriented and take the time to educate their clients about their investments.

Choosing to make smart choices with your money is an act of self-appreciation and self-worth. If you care for yourself as much as you care for anyone else in your life, you'll care for your money.

From my experience as a financial adviser, I know that once women commit to investing, they are excellent investors. Most are conservative, long-term thinkers who prefer to grow their wealth slowly over time, rather than engage in get-rich schemes. They're careful with their money and accustomed to stretching their personal and family budgets to their advantage. They're intuitive with their choices with a great sense of where to place their money. They're nurturing of their investments with their families' best interests in mind. They are cooperative and collaborative, sharing what they've learned with other women investors.

So what separates savvy women from reluctant investors?—a desire to learn, a willingness to take back ownership of their money, a hunger to be financially independent in their own right, and a commitment to put all this into practice by saving and reinvesting profits.

In $avvy Women, $mart Choices I've chosen to teach through the real-life stories of my clients. All of these women wrote their stories under assumed names and geographic locations to protect their privacy. They range in age from 25 to 94, and each one of them made a life-changing choice to start where they could and take back their financial lives. Carol performed open-air analysis on a local company to identify stock with excellent growth potential, which happens to be the mainstay of her portfolio. Dorothy, born in the 'hood, the only girl in a family of twenty-three, overcame racism and sexism to fight for her education and create a new legacy for her children and grand-children. Jennifer dodged a brainless bovine scam to become a buyer-beware investor. And Jani set up 1031 tax-deferred exchanges to trade profits from the sale of her resort property into two more properties while deferring a cool $135,000 in taxes!

Life does not stand still. Circumstances, both those within our control and those not, change. Perhaps Joy, whose story appears later, suggests our reality most lyrically: "like the river, there have been many turns in my journey."

- *Marcia VanderWoude*

PREFACE

Part One of this book highlights two financial debacles, both resulting from breaches of trust. Brigitte's story is all too common in both life and fiction. She first placed her faith in those she loved—her husband and her best friend. When they betrayed her, she put her future in the hands of lawyers and accountants. Her heart was shattered, but so was her financial security.

Victoria's story reveals the impact of professional arrogance, ambition and grandiosity on one person's life. A rising star in the investment world repeatedly assured her, "Let me worry about that." She did, and that human meteor left an enormous crater in her finances.

Part Two of this book presents the stories of women who have prudently accumulated and managed assets, many in loving partnership with a spouse who shared the same financial values. These stories illustrate the win-win possibilities of healthy interdependence versus unhealthy dependence.

Part Three of this book presents the advanced investment strategies of women who have developed not just competency but expertise in managing their assets. They are women who, step by step, moved toward complex, rewarding approaches to making the most of their options and opportunities.

It is my hope that each of you will relate to at least one woman and one smart choice, and that you will put that smart choice to work for you. If you read all the stories, you will be privy to forty-two of the smartest choices women can make in financial and estate planning. What waits for you is more freedom to live life on your terms, in balance and sync with what you've earned and what you've been given. As you find that harmony for yourself, you pave the way for other women to do the same. And as such, you perform a great service for the world, for too many women have suffered a lack of worth and money. It is to this global change that I commit this book.

"From birth until age 18, a girl needs good parents.
From 18 to 35, she needs good looks.
From 35 to 55, she needs a good personality.
From 55 on, she needs cash."

Sophie Tucker (1884 – 1966)
American entertainer

Part One:
The Case for $mart Choices

BRIGITTE: SLEEPLESS IN PARADISE

*"All changes, even the most longed for, have their
melancholy, for what we leave behind is a part of ourselves;
we must die to one life before we can enter another."*

Anatole France (1844 – 1924)
French author

I'm fifty-two and still not making a living. It's not that I'm lazy
or not working. I'm running two businesses now and have had many
jobs and other businesses, too. And I'm not blaming anyone either or
feeling victimized by anyone or any circumstance. As a matter of fact,
I feel very fortunate and blessed that I've made it as a single parent for
almost fifteen years.

Money never used to be a problem. I was born and raised in
a comfortable Belgian family, not really rich, but having more than
enough. My parents paid my tuition at boarding school and gave me
money to cover my expenses. They sent me to university to complete
my education. That's where I met my American boyfriend. We married soon after college and moved close to his family in Miami where
he attended medical school.

Women in my family never worked outside the home for a
separate income. They were homemakers and great cooks, raising

children, maintaining relationships, organizing events, and sometimes, paying the bills. I don't think my mother knew how much my
father made. I surely didn't. Plus, no one really talked about money
in our family.

So you might say that when I got married, I never expected to
have to make a living. It was the man's role and after all, I married a
future doctor. I did help in the beginning with part-time jobs, teaching French at Berlitz or working in stores until I had my first child. It
wasn't easy living away from my family in Belgium, but gradually I
adapted to the American culture. My husband and I moved four more
times so he could complete his education, before settling in
Colorado.

After fifteen years of marriage, we finally had a comfortable
life. My husband was a specialist and made excellent money. He had
paid off his education debts, invested in a retirement plan, and started college funds for both children. Like my mother, I never knew
exactly how much he made, but I trusted him totally in all financial
matters. I was on automatic pilot, managing life day to day with two
small children, and that kept me very busy and quite happy. I was
especially thrilled to be living in our new, bigger dream home.

Then suddenly, everything changed, and I never even saw it
coming. My best and only friend at the time was moving away; her
husband had lost his job, and they had to relocate. She revealed to me
that she had been having an affair with my husband for the past two
years and was in love with him. I was in shock. I felt stabbed in the
back. My life was crumbling underneath me. Divorce wasn't even a
word in my vocabulary until then—it was something that happened
to other people, but not me. I had to quickly come to terms with the
fact that my marriage was over. I was hurt, ashamed, and angry. At 40,
I had no idea who I was, what I wanted, what I needed. We had a very
bitter two-year divorce which has taken over ten years to heal.

In planning for my divorce, I had counted on my lawyers and
accountants to figure out what was best for me, which was a huge
mistake. They ended up taking better care of their fees than my financial future. I had assumed they would tell me what I needed in terms
of income, investments, health insurance, life insurance and other
considerations. I kept asking them questions, and they would tell me
we would deal with that later. After two years of preparing for our

court date, they penciled in settlement figures the night before.

I was so clueless that I had thought these were just preliminary numbers, and I would have a final say in the settlement. That's when I realized that key details were left out, such as when my ex-husband had to pay me my monthly checks. If he decided to skip a month or hold up a payment, I had little recourse under the decree. There were no provisions for my health insurance or other financial safeguards I badly needed. I never remember signing anything on my own divorce. When I reviewed my divorce papers, I asked for changes, but it was too late. The judge allowed some minor revisions, but the numbers were set.

Nothing really changed in my lifestyle at first. I kept receiving $5,000 checks (for alimony, child support, and a schooling allowance) into my bank account and felt very privileged and fortunate. I wasn't too concerned about my finances. Six months before the divorce court date, I had met a wonderful Portuguese man who adored me, boosted my self-esteem and wanted to marry me. He helped me let go of my big house, which I wanted to keep but couldn't afford with a mortgage of $3,500 a month. That house had been my only attachment to America, but when he came into the picture, I imagined my children and me moving to Portugal, nearer to my parents. So I settled my divorce with about $50,000 cash in various payments, a retirement plan of $250,000, and five years of alimony and a school allowance as well as child support. I signed the divorce papers with the idea of remarriage, so it didn't seem so bad.

Two months later, just before Christmas, my boyfriend had a car accident and broke off the relationship. I was devastated once again. By January of the following year, I hit bottom. I felt alone, depressed, and anxious, with no plans, no real friend or partner. I was going to leave my beautiful home within six months, and my ex-husband and his new wife would move in! Fortunately, one month later, my neighbor told me that someone in the neighborhood was subdividing his big lot and planned to put it on the market soon. She suggested I take a look at it. It was magic. For the first time since my separation and divorce, I had both a vision and a plan. I was going to rebuild a house and a life for myself. It felt simple and perfect.

I had never made any major financial decisions in my life and suddenly, I was making several of them at the same time. I was buying the lot, finding a builder, negotiating a bank loan, selecting materials for the interior and exterior, and serving as co-contractor on the project to save money. My father was an architect, and he drew up the plans for me, which was a tremendous support. It was an exciting time. I still had many emotional ups and downs, but I was taking pride in my house project and feeling respect for myself again.

I was winging it day by day, living in the flow. I took a variety of classes, trying to figure out what I wanted to do for the rest of my life. I took language classes, marketing and real estate, business, and psychology. My collection of books grew from *What Color is My Parachute?* to *Do What You Love & The Money Will Follow* to *The Artist's Way*, *Swim with the Sharks*, *The Four Agreements* and many more.

I graduated with a master's degree in agency counseling in 1997 and worked full time as an intern at a hospital under the supervision of a Ph.D. in psychology. It was great work experience, but I saw a dim future as a medical social worker, and there was no real money coming in yet. The early years of the divorce had lulled me into a security net that $5,000 a month would always be there, and I didn't realize how hard it was to generate that same income in the outside world.

Next I tried having my own mediation business with another psychologist, but nothing gelled. My private practice was lacking clients, so I taught some French classes and started a business selling scarves. It kept me very busy while raising my children. I was constantly juggling schedules, managing my health, and trying to keep up with my home, friends, and dates.

After ten years on my own, I was in a rut, worrying more and more about money and having bouts of depression that lasted longer every time. A minimum-wage job just wasn't an option. By January 2001 I needed to get away, so I visited some friends in San Diego and fell in love with the climate and lifestyle there. On my way home, I pictured my life back in Colorado, hidden away on a five-acre lot that I couldn't maintain, dead-end jobs, and feeling very lonely even with many friends around. I knew for my sanity that I had to make some changes.

My son had just finished middle school. I sold the house and lot and moved to San Diego for a new beginning. That was three years ago. When I arrived, I got some sales jobs while continuing to grow my business with scarves and other accessories and clothing. I sold at shows, events, and women's groups. It provided some income but not enough to get myself on solid financial footing.

For too many years now, even with reducing my lifestyle a lot, I still live way above my means. I keep hoping that something will work out soon. Maybe it's my pride that stops me from giving up my little business and wishing it would take off and grow successfully. The truth is my business has created more credit card debt than income. Instead of feeling successful, I wake up every day feeling overwhelmed with my to-do lists and more insecure about my future.

I realize now that I could have bought and sold real estate properties and invested the profits instead of working so hard to sell more accessories or trying to make ends meet with low-paying jobs. I can honestly say that I made the best choices at the time with the information I had.

I feel proud that I have raised independent and self-confident children, and they will be better prepared to meet the world than I was. At some point, I will inherit money from my parents in Belgium, but that is many years away. I really want to generate a great income on my own and feel successful without having to touch my retirement account until age sixty-five or older.

While I've learned to be in the driver's seat emotionally, physically, and spiritually, I still feel like a passenger in my financial life, along for the ride but a failure at creating my own wealth. I am open to learning all I can to turn my situation around.

ADVISER'S CORNER

I applaud Brigitte's willingness to come forward and admit her failed choices. She is open and ready to learn a better way to organize her financial life and create lasting wealth. We have already been in conversation regarding her next moves. Her youngest son graduates this year, giving her the option to scale back her living expenses even further.

I suggested she rent a one-bedroom condo for $800 a month, instead of the $1,600 a month she pays now, and save the difference toward buying her own condo. The California real estate market has held strong and actually more than doubled in the last five years (Wall Street

Journal, March 4, 2005). She also needs the stability of a salaried position with benefits to relieve her of the stress of running a business that is putting her further into debt. The risks, rewards and challenges of self-employment or small business ownership must be weighed and balanced against economic realities. Once she makes a few changes like these, she will feel more confident taking additional steps towards her financial security.

Divorce either keeps women immobilized, clinging to the status quo and waiting for things to get better, or it spurs them into a frantic search to find themselves. Each one of these changes has its own cost in time and money. I advise my younger female clients to maintain at least a part-time involvement in their careers, so they can be prepared to step back into the job market if needed.

VICTORIA: A TRAGEDY OF TRUST

"Like their personal lives, women's history is fragmented, interrupted; a shadow history of human beings whose existence has been shaped by the efforts and the demands of others."

Elizabeth Janeway (1913 –)
American author and critic

I grew up in a working-class family with four children and a stay-at-home mother. There was no money for extras or savings for the future. Father had a strong work ethic which was instilled in me. Since there was no money for higher education, I went to work immediately following high school, starting at the entry level of a major corporation. I took college classes in the evenings and earned a degree some years later. At twenty-one, I married a man without a college education. He worked in a family-owned business where wages were low and received no benefits. I took on the responsibility of being the primary breadwinner.

Over the years I worked my way up in the company to a six-figure income through dedication, hard work, long hours, and a strong work ethic. I wanted to be more secure financially than my parents, and I was driven to work hard and save. I put money in savings from the time I started working. This included a company employee stock plan, a 401K with company match, and credit-union and bank savings accounts. College funds for children were not an issue because I had chosen not to have children and to focus instead on my career. My husband continued in the struggling family business with no pension plan or benefits.

My company, along with so many others, began consolidating and downsizing and continued in that mode over the years. After twenty-seven years I decided I needed to look seriously at my options should my job be eliminated or if I opted for an early retirement. In discussions with fellow employees, I was directed to a young financial adviser with a major brokerage firm to help me explore my choices. He had done a good job for them and was impressive with his helpfulness and investment knowledge. I was a complete novice at investing, my only experience being my savings plan and 401K, the latter of which was managed through my company. I had relied on co-workers for advice on where to put my 401K dollars and had never taken a real interest in investing. I shared this background with my adviser who convinced me he would handle all my investment dealings. He was the expert; thus, I trusted him to serve me with honesty and integrity. Firms like his exist for that reason. I could now continue to focus my energies on my job and future.

I began by setting up an IRA account with this firm and broker as well as an asset account for short-term purposes. I rolled over a portion of my company 401K and sold some of my employee stock to fund these accounts initially. My approach to investing was very conservative. I told my adviser I had accumulated significant dollars and my first concern was *not to lose* what I had, but to earn more than a passbook-savings type account could earn. He indicated it was more than possible.

A couple years after I began investing with him, he moved to an even larger firm. I transferred my account with him. I felt very safe with him and this move to the new firm. Up to this time my accounts continued to grow.

After my accounts had been established, he presented different scenarios for me to handle my financial needs should I choose to take early retirement in the next couple of years or at some point prior to normal retirement age. With the pressures at work and the accomplishment of a long, successful career, I was getting ready to leave.

The adviser showed me that I already had nearly enough money accumulated, including a lump-sum pension I would receive, to live on the modest income I had projected. I also had the portion of my company 401K that I had not rolled over which was still invested. I was going to use this in the future for purposes other than retirement. I decided to retire in approximately one year and to leave my IRA untouched. I would do some type of part-time work and live on that income and savings for as long as I could, allowing my portfolio to continue to grow.

Following my plan, I retired in 1997 and rolled over my lump-sum payout to my broker's firm. My adviser handled all the paperwork and details for me, making it easy and assuring me he had invested my dollars in a diverse and conservative manner, primarily using mutual funds, since I needed to earn only about 7% on my total portfolio to have a comfortable lifestyle. I again made it clear that I needed $42,000 in income annually from this account.

During the following three years the market was very good. I did consulting work and used those earnings, as well as savings I had, for living expenses. My adviser contacted me often and assured me my investments were safe and doing well, which they were as far as I could tell from the monthly statements I received.

Beginning in early 1999, some family issues arose, and I had to stop working to care for my mother, who had major health problems. In addition, my husband and I divorced, and I had a financial settlement with him that impacted my portfolio but did not cause a problem for my retirement. I decided to begin an early withdrawal on my IRA account in the third quarter of that year. My broker worked out the numbers and decided I had enough funds to split my IRA into two IRA accounts—one to draw on and one as a backup should I need additional funds prior to fifty-nine-and-a-half years old, when I could begin withdrawing without penalty. The projection was at modest earnings of approximately 7%. Life was good.

About the time I began my early pension withdrawal, the market began its decline. I continually counseled with my broker, because I was very nervous. I had constant reassurances from him that my account was stable, my investment vehicles were conservative, and I would be okay as I was not at risk. There would be a small roller-coaster ride for a period of time, but I had nothing to worry about. I trusted him completely. However, as time went by, the market continued to slide, my funds continued to decline, and my broker quit communicating with me. When we did talk, he continued to tell me to quit worrying; he was watching the market, knew how to manage my account, and I would be fine.

As it turns out, I was not fine. I lost nearly 60% of my retirement, and at the rate I was withdrawing, I would be out of money long before I reached age sixty-five. I insisted on a meeting with my adviser when I realized what a disaster my finances really were. He continued to tell me I was not looking at the numbers correctly. He would lay it all out for me and explain it. After that meeting, I did not hear from him for almost six months, and he contacted me only after I wrote his company with my complaint and concerns.

I then had some meetings with my adviser and his managers, even exchanging letters with the company's attorneys, only to be told that I was the one responsible for my investments. They stated that the adviser's role was to give me input, but I made all the decisions. My losses were due to a declining market that impacted everyone. Furthermore, I had been aggressive in my investments.

From the first day I had met him in 1996, my adviser took over my investment decisions and had told me that's what I paid him for—he even had said I should not watch financial programs, as he was the expert. He constantly reassured me that I was invested conservatively and safely and that my retirement funds were not in jeopardy. This continued right until the time when, in a meeting with his manager, he acknowledged I did not have enough dollars to maintain my current pattern of withdrawing.

I have found myself with a ruined retirement. I am doing some part-time consulting as I find it. I have switched advisers within that firm until I can determine where I want to move my remaining funds. I no longer trust anyone in the securities arena to be honest after what I have gone through and after following all the industry scandals. I worry daily how to continue my lifestyle into the future, and I am trying to learn more about my own money management.

My only option in pursuing some recovery of my losses is through the arbitration process. This was outlined in the fine print of the materials I was given back in 1996 when I opened my initial account. I have retained an attorney to assist me in the process, which is extremely complex.

The industry tells investors the arbitration process is much simpler than a court proceeding, since an attorney is really not needed, and it is much quicker. My experience has been just the opposite. The process is complex, extremely time-consuming, and as about as easy to maneuver through as the new prescription drug process for the elderly. An attorney is a must since the brokerage firm uses its own attorneys.

It has been nearly two years since I filed my formal complaint.

Arbitration Update (February 2005)

There is no way a person should go through arbitration without counsel. The brokerage firm has been represented by a slick, high-powered attorney who specializes in arbitrations. The average investor is no match for that.

I am a seasoned manager, an executive with years of experience in conflict resolution, and this has been the most challenging situation I've ever encountered. I thought that I'd be talking about my retirement account, but the firm's attorney has lumped all my assets and financial decisions together, trying to show that I am more sophisticated in money matters than I am revealing. He is going into great depth about my spending patterns with other accounts—checking and savings—that the brokerage firm never handled. I had to disclose six years' worth of financial information prior to my investing in their firm: tax returns, bank statements, etc.

I've already spent $7,000 in copies and notebooks for the three arbitrators. This does not include my attorney's fees which will likely be a percentage of the final recovery settlement, if any. It has been overwhelming, way beyond what I expected I would have to do. I feel like a criminal gone to court, pronounced guilty.

The firm's attorney is also insisting that since my complaint is taking more time than usual because of the way I'm presenting my case, that I should have to pay a higher percentage of the arbitration costs, usually split 50-50. This seems grossly unfair that as an individual I may be asked to pay more than my share of an arbitration necessitated by the firm's negligence.

I can see why people don't do this. I'm just so stubborn that I won't give up. I have learned that this adviser has ruined at least six other retirement accounts, and I would like the arbitrators to hold him accountable in my case.

My arbitration has now been extended another three months to April at which time I will resume the fight to recover some of the losses in my ruined retirement account.

Arbitration Lost (April 2005)

I have lost my arbitration! Both my attorney and I are a bit amazed but not really surprised. We felt the scales were weighted in their favor all along. This has certainly set me back and made it necessary to retool my life. My past thirty years of saving, saving, saving are down the drain. I guess I have only myself to blame. In addition to the money I have already spent on this case, my attorney tells me they have ruled I owe NASD (National Association of Securities Dealers) another $11,300 in costs. Plus, per the rules, I get no explanation of why the ruling went the way it did.

Having gone through this nearly three-year journey and getting educated in the world of investing, I sincerely believe the rules governing investment professionals, as well as the arbitration process itself, are biased and not designed to protect or help unsophisticated, common investors. I do not think most individuals really could understand the process of going through arbitration without significant study. The reality of challenging an individual broker and/or his firm with any chance of success, not to mention the cost involved and definite need for an attorney's help, is a joke. Without my attorney, I would have been alone, pitted against the high-powered, expensive legal team of my brokerage firm, a team that specializes in these cases.

I believe there is a need for major reform in this process, especially in light of proposed changes to Social Security and individual retirement accounts. I am afraid of how many people could be hurt financially. I know the general population does not understand things like *discretionary* and *non-discretionary* brokerage accounts, for example. And, while the forms a person signs when setting up an account use these terms in very fine print by the signature line, brokers generally do not explain them and most people don't read the fine print, let alone the prospectus for the investment fund. How many people are truly ready, willing, and able to embrace reform and take back ownership of their money and retirement?

After this extended battle, I need some time to decompress, heal, and regroup. I hope other women can learn from my experience and be the wiser for it.

ADVISER'S CORNER

This tragic story demonstrates the importance of finding an appropriate financial adviser who clearly understands your goals and objectives, implements suitable investments for your life stage and risk tolerance, educates you completely on these investments, and has no discretionary power over your accounts.

There were several red flags here—not returning phone calls, blaming a declining market, bringing in the "old boys' club" of managers to back him up, and telling Victoria that he didn't want her to watch financial programs because he was the expert.

*An adviser who has your best interests in mind helps you make informed decisions about your investments and communicates openly and freely. There is nothing to hide, no one to blame, no games to be played. Victoria was close to retirement and should not have been put in aggressive investments. If she had been my client, I would have placed 95% of her portfolio in **laddered treasury** and high-quality corporate bonds. She would have had a 6–8% cash flow to live on and have all of her principal intact today.*

Part Two:
Basic Strategies

KRISTY: TOOL BELTS FOR TWO

"The secret of getting ahead is getting started."

Agatha Christie (1890 – 1976)
American author

Growing up, I rarely had to worry about money. We were not rich or poor, but middle class. My father worked full-time, and my mother raised us and did some part-time work once we were in high school.

My father gave me a credit card to use since I did a lot of the grocery and supply shopping. When I completed college, I decided to live on my own. I got an apartment with my boyfriend Jake, who was almost two years older than I and is now my husband. We had met just after I graduated from high school while Jake was in his first year of college.

Once we were moved into the apartment, my dad said, "Okay it's time to give me back my credit card, so you can live on your own." He took me by surprise. I thought living on my own I would still get to keep his credit card. Reluctantly, I returned the card, and my boyfriend and I set out to make it on our own.

Jake and I purchased our first house six months before our wedding in a very popular city about forty-five minutes north of

Detroit. We repainted the inside, took out the carpet on the first floor, finished the existing hardwood floors, rebuilt the deck, and put tile in the kitchen and breakfast nook. Jake also built a bar that overlooked the family room, and we changed all of the fixtures and knobs to silver. After living in the house for one year, I was transferred to the west side of the state. We sold the house in twenty-one days and made 20% profit over our initial investment.

Our second house was purchased because of its proximity to the expressway, since Jake was still planning to keep his job on the other side of the state. It was a nice, brand-new house in a three-year-old subdivision scheduled to be completed by the end of that year. We purchased all the appliances, built a deck, and put in a lawn and landscaping. We gave the same love and attention to detail as we had given to our first house. This time, when we decided to sell, the house was on the market for six months before we accepted an offer for 7% more than our purchase price. We learned that appreciation potential was greater for older fixer-uppers like our first house than newer homes like our second house.

We are currently renovating our third house, a unique property in a beautiful subdivision with very large, old trees. So far, we have repainted every room, switched the lighting fixtures, knobs, and fans, installed a new hot tub, and built a deck around it. My husband is working on a new sauna, which should be finished soon. We have many more projects planned, including installing new wood or stone floors in the hallway and living room, re-carpeting the bedrooms, building a new master bathroom, and adding to the existing basement bathroom. We have lived here just six months, and the house has increased in value about 15% since we had our first appraisal.

Because we had to close on this house before we sold our second home, we had to pay two monthly mortgage payments, not something we planned or wanted to do this early in our lives. However, we look at this house as an investment opportunity, and that was a risk we were willing to take. After taking my parents through our third house, they offered to help us if we needed money. They also thought this was a solid investment and realized how much we loved this house. Our goal is to own a beach home on the west coast of Michigan, and with the profits we're making from the sales of these homes, we are well on our way.

ADVISER'S CORNER

What I appreciate about Kristy and Jake is their passion for getting started. I remember the first time I met them, I was astounded at how socially mature and astute they were. They had great instincts regarding which properties to buy, were able to budget their finances to cover the mortgage(s), and had the combined talent to do the remodeling themselves.

As young people in their mid-twenties, they do not yet have the financial responsibility of raising children, so they are free to reinvest all their profits in their next real estate purchase. With the discipline they've mastered in renovating three homes, I am sure they will be able to balance new responsibilities and still reach their goal of owning a beach home.

$MART CHOICE

Renovating a House

- Purchase undervalued property in an area with great appreciation potential

- Do research up-front regarding the neighborhood, recent selling prices of comparable homes, zoning and city planning

- Purchase properties with good bones (basic structure) that need primarily cosmetic improvements (paint, tile, carpet, landscaping, etc.)

- Get tips on techniques from stores like Home Depot or Lowe's and shows like "Extreme Makeover"

- Avoid "over-improving;" features and materials should not be excessive for neighborhood

- Save money by doing the work yourself

- Reinvest the profits into your next fixer-upper

DENICE: PRIMED TO SAVE

*"One's prime is elusive. You little girls, when you grow up,
must be on the alert to recognize your prime at whatever time
of your life it may occur. You must then live it to the full."*

Muriel Spark (1918 –)
British author

I learned financial responsibility throughout my life by listening to the conversations my parents, Marie and William, had with one another and with me. They told me to avoid debt except to buy a house, to invest in an education or to make a short-term purchase such as a car. Continually warned about the danger of credit cards, I did not have one of my own until I married at age twenty-one. I did not have a checkbook or debit card until college.

The value of money was fixed in my mind by having to use cash and seeing the money leave my hands rather than just signing a piece of paper. That really made a big impression. I began budgeting in late elementary school and junior high when I wanted to buy name-brand clothing costing more than the amount my parents gave me. It made me more aware of what clothing truly cost, and I had to ask myself if it was worth paying extra for a fancy name.

As a teenager, I earned money in my parents' company—it

was not just given to me. When I began working for them, they opened a **Roth IRA** for me. I did not understand a lot about it then, except that I was saving money and contributing to it. My parents had insisted that I save 10% of every paycheck and since I did this routinely, it became both a habit and instilled value.

When I went off to college and managed my own financial accounts, I became more interested in reading books about how to invest. I learned that it is more beneficial to invest a small amount sooner and regularly rather than a larger amount infrequently or later. Since my parents taught me so much about investing and set up the Roth for me, I was able to contribute faithfully to it at the beginning of each year.

I am also fortunate my husband and I have shared values about saving. He is currently a medical resident and because he works long hours, he does not have the time to speak to a financial adviser and review investments. We agreed that he would give me **power of attorney** to make investment decisions for him. This streamlines our saving and keeps our investments on track. My husband trusts me implicitly, and we have been able to fund Roth IRAs for both of us as well as set up a college savings plan for our new baby.

It can be hard when you are young and think you have no money to invest, but time is on our side. My parents continue to educate us financially, and I hope I can do as well with our children.

ADVISER'S CORNER

Denice is an excellent saver and has always lived well within her means. Because of her commitment to investing, she will be assured a comfortable retirement. It's rare to find twenty-year-olds already engaged in retirement savings. I encouraged her to read additional financial books and learn advanced investment strategies.

The Roth IRA was a smart choice, because it offers fewer restrictions about withdrawal. But by far, her smartest choice was obtaining power of attorney for her husband's investments. It would have been easy to leave the investing to him, and he might or might not have gotten around to it. Savvy women don't wait—they take responsibility for their financial futures.

$MART CHOICES

Roth IRA

- Created in 1996 by an act of Congress

- Contributions are:
  - Non-deductible
  - Non-taxable when withdrawn

- Gains must stay in the Roth until age 59½ and the account has been held for five years

- Penalty-free withdrawals can be taken in case of disability or death

- Income limitations:
  - Modified adjusted gross income must be less than $110,000 for a single taxpayer or $160,000 for married taxpayers
  - Maximum contribution for 2005 is $4,000 per year for those under age 50, and $4,500 for those over age 50

Power of Attorney

- Legal document authorizing a person to make legal and financial decisions for another person while that person is alive

- Designated person is *agent* or *attorney-in-fact*

LYDIA: THE GOOD STEWARD

"Self-preservation is the first responsibility."

Margaret Anderson (1886 – 1973)
American literary editor and autobiographer

I come from a tradition of savers and conservative spenders. My grandparents were immigrants who survived the Depression, and the lessons they learned from that experience were passed on to my parents and us children. We were taught to appreciate what we had and to manage it as a precious resource.

My parents both worked outside the home. Dad was an engineer, and Mom went back to college to earn a second master's degree when I was in high school. She then returned to full-time work as a special education teacher. At the time, it was unusual for mothers to work outside the home. My parents valued education and had set a goal to fund college for their three girls.

As a child, I had opened my first passbook savings account at the local bank with a small deposit of seven dollars. That taught me the value of saving. Later, I supplemented my weekly allowance with babysitting jobs. I got my first real job at the bookstore the summer after I graduated from high school. Throughout college I worked about ten hours a week in the college library.

I received a fellowship to graduate school, where I earned both a master's and doctoral degree in English. I married a fellow educator while still in grad school and worked several years after completing my degrees. We had a son but unfortunately divorced a few years later. I have always been able to maintain a good relationship with my ex-husband; together we have been committed to raising our son and providing the best for him.

When I became a professor, I was able to join **TIAA-CREF**, a retirement fund for college teachers. During the years my son was growing up, there were tuition expenses for his education. I was not able to add to my retirement savings except for a $2,000 annual contribution to an IRA account and a small contribution in each paycheck to a tax-deferred annuity account.

Once my son was on his own, I began saving in earnest. I converted my IRA to a Roth IRA and was able to take advantage of the over-50 catch-up provision to both my Roth IRA and my 403B account, which I opened with TIAA-CREF. Although this reduces my salary nearly in half, I like the discipline of learning to live on less.

Recently, after a comeback in the stock market, I moved about two-thirds of my TIAA-CREF funds into the fixed account. My goal is to put enough into the TIAA-CREF account so that earnings from that account, in addition to projected income from Social Security, should cover my basic expenses during retirement. I will continue some investment in stock funds and bond funds to provide additional income for retirement activities such as travel and the pursuit of my hobbies: quilting, knitting, and gardening.

As a product of the '60s, I've always had an independent spirit and a strong desire to make it on my own. I enjoy doing things by hand, from canning tomatoes to making my own clothes. I am looking forward to the flexibility of retirement and hope to pursue activities with my friends who share similar interests.

To me stewardship means making the most of the resources I've been given and refusing to waste money, time, and talents. I can honestly reflect on my life thus far and feel satisfied that I have done just that.

ADVISER'S CORNER

Lydia, now in her late fifties, is a dream client. She goes online and prints out monthly statements of her accounts, meets semi-annually with me to review her asset allocation, and saves the maximum for her retirement. I project that she will be able to retire as much as three years ahead of schedule due to her rigorous saving and her goal of paying off her mortgage. She has sacrificed a lot in her personal lifestyle to contribute to her retirement, which is rare indeed in this age of living beyond one's means.

 # $MART CHOICE

TIAA-CREF

- *TIAA-CREF stands for Teachers Insurance and Annuity Association—College Retirement Equities Fund* and is a $300 billion financial services company with 3.2 million participants

- Program is available at 97% of US colleges and universities

- Open to college teachers, employees at Mayo Clinic, Ford Foundation, and some other institutions

- **TIAA** invested in fixed income investments since 1918

- **CREF** invested in equity (stock) investments since 1952

- Thirty-two different fund choices for 2005

- Maximum contribution for 2005 is $14,000 per year for those under age 50 or $18,000 for those over age 50

JULIA: STOCK MARKET AFICIONADO

"One faces the future with one's past."

Pearl S. Buck (1892 – 1973)
American author

I'd like to be able to tell you that my family had a positive influence on my finances, but the truth is, they didn't. My father always had difficulty saving. Money just seemed to burn a hole in his pocket, as it had with my grandfather before him. When he and mom first married, he owned a prosperous landscaping business and earned a few extra dollars on the side by buying used cars, fixing them up, and reselling them. But instead of saving this money, he'd take the family out to dinner. Years later he broke his back and could no longer run his landscaping business. Idle for a year, he got an office job, and mother took over the family budget.

Seeing my father struggle with money, I was more determined than ever to do things differently. I knew my parents couldn't pay for college, and I didn't qualify for scholarships, so I set some goals for myself. I worked two summers before graduation from high school and saved all the money I made. In 1961 I purchased a '51 Chevy, which enabled me to attend a small college in Iowa for my freshman year. Then I transferred to another college in Missouri for my sophomore year. That's when I ran out of money, even though I worked part-time in the cafeteria. I decided to borrow money from my grand-mother to finish out the year.

I spent the next year at an unfulfilling job as a typist, and this only renewed my desire to complete college. People told me, "Once you have a taste of earning money, you will never go back to college," but I didn't feel that way. Because I didn't enjoy my job, I saved like crazy to get back to school. I sold my car, repaid my grandmother, and went back to finish my degree. I worked two jobs in the summer, one as a camp counselor and another as a gas company employee. During the school year, I played tennis for the university, but still no scholarships were available. By the time I graduated debt-free with a B.A. in sociology, I felt like I had truly accomplished a major life goal.

My first job was program director for teens at a small YWCA. The salary was only $5,000 a year, but because I had learned to live on a meager income and still save throughout college, I made the most of what I had. In 1967, the year of race riots, I found inspiration in working with people who had marched with Dr. Martin Luther King. As a social worker, I've always made below average salary, but have been paid in human capital as well as real dollars. The early dis-cipline of saving has enabled me to slowly build up some cash.

My banker suggested that I go to a major brokerage firm to invest some of my savings for a greater return on my investment. I began working with an adviser who recommended a few **growth stocks**. I found that the bold strokes of the stock market were a great match for my love of risk taking and charting my own course.

One stock that I purchased eventually doubled, and the advis-er suggested that I take my profits and sell. I decided to hold, think-ing it would keep going higher. When the stock crashed, I learned my lesson and began to temper my bold strokes with more conservative investment strategies. That's when I chose to put my retirement plans in **Class A Mutual Funds**, for they were a more diversified portfolio of stocks, bonds, and cash, spreading the risk among several growth stocks instead of one.

I am very interested in the stock market and love to theorize about which stocks will move up and down. When I work with my adviser, I prefer to be actively involved in selecting my stocks and read all I can about various stocks' performance as well as current economic conditions. Most of the times, my instincts are right on and my assets have grown steadily over the years. But I continue to remain humbled by that first major loss and also rely on the advice of my broker.

As a single woman, I am well aware that I need to provide for myself and my own retirement. Those risks I took as a young woman have paid off as I've created a more secure financial future for myself.

ADVISER'S CORNER

Growth stocks are a great match for investors who are risk takers, but there will be losses as well as gains with this more speculative choice of investment. If an investor wants to hold a stock that, in my opinion, should be sold, I usually advise her to sell half and keep half. That way she can protect herself if the stock drops, by taking some profit, and she can keep her position in the company if she still likes the stock.

Class A Mutual Funds are a long-term holding, as there is a front-end load (commission) built into the buying price. They are typically more conservative than growth stocks as they spread the risk over several growth stocks within the fund versus one growth stock which may or may not perform well. Class A Mutual Funds also have lower expense ratios (or annual costs to operate the fund: administrative costs, commissions, etc.) built into the price, reflected in the net performance numbers of the fund.

$MART CHOICES:

Growth Stocks

- Stocks (or ownership shares) in a company that's growing rapidly or aggressively

- Primary objective is to grow share price rather than pay out dividends to shareholders

- Usually high stock price relative to what the company earns

- No dividends or very small dividends paid to shareholders

- Earnings get reinvested back into the company

- Profits grow, and stock price usually goes up

Class A Mutual Fund

- Any type of mutual fund invested in stocks, bonds, or cash

- Sold in shares referred to as Class A shares

- Has a *front-end load* (commission) built into the share price, payable to the broker at the time of purchase (usually 4–5% commission)

- No commission paid on the back end of a transaction when selling the shares

LYNN: THE LAND BARONESS

*"I have learned you have to trust yourself, be what you are,
and do what you ought to do the way you should do it.
You have got to discover you, what you do, and trust it."*

Barbara Streisand (1942 –)
American singer, actress, and director

Some people have lofty goals of what they want to achieve in life. I am content living on the land my parents owned before me, a beautiful wooded property complete with its own Walden Pond, several deer, wild turkeys, and other wildlife. When I awake in the morning, I call the deer to me and they come out of the clearing to eat corn from my hands. I have a special name for each of them. This land has always been my home, my refuge.

Developers are anxious to buy my property, projecting it will triple in value over the next twenty years. I am in no hurry to sell. Now that I am retired, I could use some additional income, so I would consider selling a few acres to the right buyer, someone who would buy it on my terms with the provision that he could not develop it for several years. I do not want my precious deer forced from the land, and I wish to keep my haven intact.

My parents had the wisdom to purchase **vacant land**, 103

acres near two resort towns in the early 1950s and ten acres some time later. The purchase price was about $30,000. They sold the ten-acre parcel for $25,000 in the early 1960s and another eighty-acre parcel for $160,000 in the 1980s. We kept the remaining twenty-three acres.

While my parents were alive, we lived in the family home on this land and I have happy memories of our time together. When they became ill, I cared for them and secured a **home equity line** to pay for their medical expenses and finance a few home improvements. The land has always been our financial security and provided well for us.

My property recently appraised for $585,000 and is projected to be worth $1.5+ million in the next twenty years. It is located near two excellent golf courses and would be prime land to develop into upper-end homes.

I have recently been in conversation with my financial adviser who told me I have several options regarding my property. I could sell it for a lump sum now and put it in income-producing investments with the provision that I could remain on the land until my death. I could sell it on a land contract in which I carry the paper for the transaction and the buyer pays me principal and interest monthly over a period of years. I could also donate it to a charity, remain on the land, and receive a yearly income based on the value of the property. There is much to consider.

When the Native Americans made decisions, they tried to consider the needs of the people seven generations out. I am a single woman with no heirs, so I do not think of the children and grandchildren who will come after me. I do, however, have reverence for the land, the wildlife, and my family home. I know I will be guided to the right decision as I continue to live on this very special land

ADVISER'S CORNER

I have advised Lynn to look for a buyer that would be able to allow her to live in the house for her lifetime and develop the property later.

Purchasing Lynn's land would be an ideal investment for a younger investor or a group of investors who could play the waiting game for the property to appreciate. It is a long-term holding, as Lynn will not allow the buyer(s) to develop the property until her death. Lynn's love of

the land is definitely a key factor in her investment choice. She has many options to remain on the property and generate the income she needs to live.

 # $MART CHOICES

Vacant Land

- Generally considered to be a long-term holding

- Best land investments located in or near resort areas, with potential for upper-end residential and/or commercial development

- Buyer should do research up front regarding zoning, city planning, development restrictions, which may affect future valuation

---

Home Equity Line of Credit

- Bank loan secured against the equity in your home

- Minimal administrative cost and little or no closing costs

- Interest rate is usually variable (prime + a margin, depending on credit score)

- Interest is tax-deductible

- Amount one can borrow (loan-to-value) depends on the property value and debt-to-income ratio of the individual

- Up to 80% of the appraised value may be borrowed depending on loan program

- May pay interest only or principal and interest

- Borrower should check pre-payment penalties, if any, before selling property or closing the line before the term of the loan expires

CAROL: SAVVY STOCK SELECTOR

"Because I am a woman, I must make unusual efforts to succeed.
If I fail, no one will say, 'She doesn't have what it takes.'
They will say, 'Women don't have what it takes.'"

Clare Boothe Luce (1903 – 1987)
American dramatist, congresswoman, and ambassador to Brazil

I was raised in an overly conservative economic atmosphere. Throughout my formative years I learned that the only acceptable debt was a mortgage and never to go into debt beyond that. My parents paid $4,000 cash for a house in the early 1940s. Our family— mother, father, three siblings—always lived comfortably within our means and saved money on a regular basis.

My father was a jack-of-all-trades. He finished high school at the age of seventy and spent his last years as a cook at a veterans' facility. He invested his savings in bonds and certificates of deposit, which I inherited when he died.

When my father's bonds matured, I started investing in Stryker, a local company based in my hometown which manufactures surgical and medical products. I had read several reports about this company in my local newspaper and had a strong intuitive sense that this would be an excellent growth company. My reasoning was that with the aging Baby Boomer population, this company would do well over a period of years. The stock has been a gold mine for me, and I continue to increase my shares in the company.

Because I taught in parochial schools, my income was very low, yet my childhood training had taught me how to save on what I earned. This discipline paid off. My husband and I have just moved into our resort home. I am now teaching in a large public school which provides me with more income, and my plan is to teach for another five years until the age of sixty-five. Because of my success with Stryker and other investments, I feel comfortable investing my 403B retirement plan in very aggressive stocks. I recently wrote and self-published a book, have had my first grandchild, and am thoroughly enjoying my very blessed life.

ADVISER'S CORNER

As Carol's adviser, I encouraged her to keep following her instincts regarding local companies. It was my job to present other companies to her that would have great investment potential for her portfolio. She was very diligent in reading the reports I gave her and in doing her own research. She did diversify her holdings by adding bank stocks and other growth stocks. However, Stryker remained her biggest and best investment because she trusted her own intuition.

When I coach women investors, I have learned to spend as much time listening to their instincts as I do presenting financial products to them. I want them to feel comfortable with their choices and empowered to trust their intuition.

$MART CHOICE

Open-Air Analysis

- *Open-air analysis,* a term coined by Peter Lynch, is the process of using one's intuition and observation to identify stock in a good local company with growth potential

- Monitor the company through articles in the newspaper, word on the street, company events

- Invest for the long term if the company is prosperous

KAYLY: 'KAY'PABILITY PERSONIFIED

"Whatever women do they must do twice as well as men to be thought half as good. Luckily, this is not difficult."

Charlotte Whitton (1896 – 1975)
Social worker and mayor of Ottawa

The women in my life, my mother and grandmothers, were excellent role models. They were all independent, capable women whether they worked in the home or outside at other jobs. Most were homemakers devoted to their families. My grandmothers lived to be ninety-four and ninety-seven years of age, and my mother is still alive at ninety-one.

Working to earn money was considered a virtue in my family. We lived next door to my maternal grandparents who had a farm and an apple orchard with a cider mill. One of my first jobs was picking up apples from the ground and placing them in wooden bushel containers which were to then to be picked up by another worker on the tractor. These apples were used to make cider. I was around ten years of age then and was paid 5¢ a bushel. This work later progressed into sorting apples and selling both cider and apples at the orchard.

I was also taught how to save money for particular goals. At age thirteen, I desperately wanted to see Elvis Presley. There was going to be an organized bus trip to the Detroit area to an Elvis concert. The total cost for the trip was $30, which also included a box lunch. Much to my parents' surprise, I saved the money prior to the trip. My grandmother didn't want me to go alone, so she paid for my cousin, who was one year older, to go with me. This did not sit well with me because I had worked long and hard to earn the money, but I got over the injustice. Undoubtedly, it taught me one of life's many lessons: that the world is not always fair, so learn to live and work within it. I did enjoy having my cousin along on the trip, and I will never forget the experience.

At age fifteen, I got what I considered to be my first real job, wrapping Christmas gifts at an upscale women's clothing store. I had to obtain a special work permit because I was less than sixteen. After the holidays, the store asked me to work part-time weekends, holidays, and summer breaks from school. This job continued throughout high school.

I attended a state university for my bachelor's degree and always managed to find a summer job. At various times I worked at a state unemployment agency, as an aide for a summer-school class, and as an assistant at the National Council on Alcoholism. My area of study was social work, so these were good internship experiences.

When I graduated from college, I returned to my parents' house because I had not yet found a job. It never occurred to me that most social work positions were in government agencies, and I didn't want to work for the government. So I decided to substitute teach to have some income. I realized that I could do plenty of social work in the schools, and I truly enjoyed working with the children. Although I did not have a teaching certificate, I was offered a teaching position and began working to obtain my certificate.

Now gainfully employed, I was able to move in with a roommate. I taught for the next two academic years and spent the summers in education courses and student teaching. I obtained my teaching certificate and secured a permanent position in a different school district for the next fall.

After teaching that year, I went through the struggling teacher's routine of finding summer work, something I was quite accustomed to. I have never been short on ambition. I found an apartment that I could afford in a newly developing community. I aggressively approached management for a summer job as a social director for the complex. Since they had not constructed the clubhouse or swimming pool yet, justification for this position was a hard sell. Instead, they hired me as a rental agent, which ultimately turned out to be pivotal in my career.

By summer's end when I was to return to school, I suggested to the management that I would be able to continue to work ten to fifteen hours a week on a rental accounting program I had assisted in setting up that summer. This part-time job continued for the next three years, and as the parent company grew, so did my work load. Eventually I was working two full-time jobs, and I had to make a decision. I loved teaching and working with children, but I found the work at the apartment complex much more challenging and interesting. It also offered me more flexibility than the classroom did.

It was at this time that I met and married my husband who had started an apartment development business. My work evolved into handling all the property management for the company, while my husband handled the construction and financial aspects of the business. As our company grew, I did much of the hiring at the corporate office. My husband accused me of hiring babies, very young people in key positions. In retrospect, this was a wise move. Almost half of the corporate office today is staffed by these individuals, who rose up through the ranks to hold high-level positions. One thing I learned early on was to surround myself with good people.

After fourteen years of marriage when I was forty-six my husband died suddenly, and I was devastated. Fortunately, I had always handled most of our personal business, and we had an efficient and loyal staff in our corporate office. The six employees had a combined total of ninety years of service with the company. I did not want to make any quick decisions about the business, and with this capable staff I had time to decide.

There was demand for more apartment units in the areas in which we were located. I decided to continue on with the business. With this able and willing staff, we built another 600 apartment units during a six-year period. Following that time I decided not to pursue additional construction. Management of about 4,000 apartment units was work enough.

I learned much about the corporate world during this period. The nature of this business was, and still is, dominated by men. Therefore, a woman has to work extra hard to break through common stereotypes. I also learned that I should do what I do best—build and manage units—and hire professionals to do the rest.

Throughout our marriage I knew that these apartments were our retirement. It is one of the reasons I worked so hard to maintain and nurture them. I had brought my own financial portfolio into the marriage and competently maintained it, but I always knew that this business was our most important asset. Because I wanted to devote most of my time to our company, I sought out the help of a financial adviser to assist with my portfolio. I decided to open and fund a **401K plan** for my employees to reward them for their ongoing loyalty and to help them secure their own retirements. I have never forgotten that our success has come largely from their hard work and high level of commitment.

The women in my family taught me to be self-reliant, to stand tall and strong in the face of adversity, and to believe in my own capabilities. This is what I pass on to the women in my company, to always stay abreast of their financial position whether they are married or not.

ADVISER'S CORNER

I admire Kayly for the great woman she is. She has made many strategic moves in her career to develop her expertise in commercial development. She entered her marriage with a portfolio in place, fully prepared to be a financial contributor in her own right. When her husband died, she courageously took over the reins of the business they had grown together.

Kayly's decision to set up a 401K for her employees is a smart investment in human capital—employees are more likely to stay when they have a vested interest in their retirement and their employer is matching contributions. It is also a wise move for Kayly, as she can fully fund a retirement plan for herself, since her primary holdings, the apartment buildings, are not liquid assets.

$MART CHOICE

401K Plan

- Voluntary retirement savings plan offered within a corporation or a company, to which employees may contribute a percentage of their pre-tax earnings

- Participant must be at least 21 and have worked one full year in the company to qualify

- Plan allows employees to contribute pre-tax earnings through payroll deductions and defer tax on income invested

- Employer may offer to match the employee's contribution

- Employers' contribution is limited to 25% of each employee's eligible salary

- Maximum contribution for 2005 is 100% of salary or $14,000, whichever is less, $18,000 if over 50

- Total contributions to any employee's fund may not go over $42,000

- Employer must offer to all qualified employees and cannot discriminate in favor of highly compensated employees

- 401K plans may be offered to employees of non-profit organizations but not to government employees

- Plan is usually set up with a mutual fund company and can be invested in stocks and bonds

KELLY: THE BIG PICTURE

*"Parents can only give good advice or put children on the right paths,
but the final forming of a person's character lies in her own hands."*

Anne Frank (1929 – 1945)
German diarist

Raised in a low-income farm family, I was taught the virtues of hard work and self-reliance and the importance of education. I was expected to go to college and never questioned how it would be paid for. I knew that if I wanted to achieve this goal, I'd have to become an active participant in my future. So I applied and received scholarships and grants and worked several part-time jobs to pay my educational expenses without going into debt.

My college had a rule that to have a job on campus students had to live in a dormitory. When I was a senior about to be married, I applied to work on campus and live off campus with my husband. The placement officer denied this, saying, "Your folks or your husband will help you out." I responded that my parents were unable to and that I wouldn't expect help from my husband. The placement officer pulled my financial record and, embarrassed and amazed, said, "How did you make it this far?" He found an on-campus placement for me, and I graduated debt-free.

Early in our marriage when we were both employed at universities, my husband managed the finances. After our only child was born, my husband was diagnosed with a chronic incurable disease. His illness forced us to reorganize our work lives and finances, and I took the lead as the breadwinner in the family. Fortunately, my husband was comfortable with this because he is a very secure man.

This was a pivotal time for me, as I realized that I would not be quitting work to stay home and raise my child. I saw my career as an investment to be continually fostered and nurtured, and I began pursuing more responsible positions for higher pay.

My husband and I managed our resources together, and I computerized our financial records so we could more easily review our investments and engage in more strategic planning. Once a year we visit our financial adviser, and I have all my financial data on spreadsheets. My husband leaves the details to me but wants to be apprised of the big picture.

Because my husband is uninsurable with his illness, our adviser suggested that we invest in some tax-deferred **annuities** that, similar to life insurance, have a death benefit but do not require a physical exam. These have become an integral part of our investment portfolio.

Today, I would not be the director of a major university program if it weren't for that decision years ago to keep my eye on the bigger picture and truly see my career as one of my most important investments.

ADVISER'S CORNER

Kelly's strong suit is that she knows about her investments at all times. She always has her finger on where she stands. Annuities are contracts with insurance companies, bought with surrender periods such as three, five, or ten years, that pay either a fixed or variable rate of return and have a death benefit attached. If the investor sells the annuity before the surrender period ends, she pays a surrender charge of 1–10% of the investment. If the investor waits until the surrender period ends, there is no charge. Partial withdrawals of 10–15% of the annuity may also be taken every year without surrender charges.

Annuities are an effective hedge against market fluctuations *because the death benefit will be the face amount or higher. I had one client who invested $45,000 in an annuity that devalued to $31,000 in a market crash, yet she continued to hold onto the investment. At the time of her death, her heirs were entitled to a $46,000 death benefit, slightly higher than her initial investment, with no loss due to the market fluctuation.*

Because of Kelly's husband's uninsurability, annuities are wise options.

$MART CHOICE

Annuities

- Investment contracts with insurance companies purchased with surrender periods such as three, five, and ten years

- Insurance company guarantees a certain rate of return or minimum interest rate

- Earnings and growth are tax deferred until withdrawn

- May be invested in fixed-rate or in variable-rate stock funds

- Surrender charge of 1–10% if investor sells annuity before maturity date

- May be used as life insurance for uninsurable people since do not require a physical exam

- May be used as life insurance because death benefit attached

LAUREN AND CLAIRE: A TALE OF TWO SISTERS

"To tend, unfailingly, unflinchingly, towards a goal, is the secret of success."

Anna Pavlova (1882 – 1931)
Russian ballerina

Lauren

We were brought up in an affluent household but were not really aware of it. Dad worked in his father's manufacturing company, and we lived very well yet were not overindulged with credit cards or cars. Mom handled the finances in the household, because Dad had no interest in them.

We learned that if you could not pay for it, you did not get it. You always paid your bills in full—no "on time" stuff. That philosophy is the one thing that has helped me the most in life.

Dad, an alcoholic, stopped drinking when Claire and I were still young and our older sister and brother were in high school. When he went into rehab, it was a lesson in money for all of us. His father had cut off his paycheck, and we had to use Dad's pension money to live while he was away for about six to eight months. In a way, we got a feel for the "other side of the tracks." For transportation we had an old, gray used car; Mom made some of our clothes, and there were no extravagances. It was a very good learning experience, though we didn't much like it when we were going through it.

Years later, Mom received an inheritance from our grandfather who had invested in the **value stocks** of companies like Standard Oil, Texaco, Bristol Myers, and General Electric. She set up an account for herself and split the remainder among the four of us children. Since this was a gift from our family, I thought it was especially important to save it and be smart with it. I kept my records in a little green book before I had a computer. I rarely spent money on myself but enjoyed spending it on others. Even when I married, I told my husband very little about my inheritance. I certainly did not want him marrying me for the money.

Mom was always a positive role model in managing money. She could have splurged on anything she wanted, yet she continued to save. She followed the stock market every day and encouraged us to be long-term investors. She introduced me to a financial adviser who suggested **selling covered calls**, which allowed me to make even more money on my stocks. Throughout the years I have continued to preserve the principal and reinvest my profits, and now my initial investment has grown to a sizeable portfolio.

Because I have had the money for so long and it was a gift from Mom, I hold my savings and investments dear to my heart. I am in this for the long haul!

ADVISER'S CORNER

Lauren has held most of these value stocks for 30+ years since her grandfather died when she was a teenager. She works closely with her accountant each year to decide when to take gains and losses in her portfolio. She is an ideal investor because she is consistently saving and reinvesting profits and dividends over time, and for the most part, she doesn't worry too much when the market goes down.

The cost basis on her inherited stocks is low because it is the price of the stocks at the time of her grandfather's death. As prices have increased on these stocks, she has made large profits and reinvested them.

Also, many of her stocks have split, creating a lower cost basis as well—
for example, 100 shares of a $50 stock split to 200 shares of a $25 stock.
    I taught Lauren how to make additional income by selling cov-
ered calls, which is like renting her stocks out for the option of selling
them at a higher price. In that case she makes money three ways: on the
stock's dividends, the option premium, and the profits from the sale of the
stocks. This is actually a very conservative investment strategy permitted
for pension funds and IRA accounts.

 # $MART CHOICES

Value Stocks

- Undervalued stocks in a good company with strong earnings, intrinsic value, sales, and cash flow

- Profits can be higher since stock is undervalued at time of purchase

- Best to reinvest dividends and profits to grow holdings over time

---

Selling Covered Calls

- Strategy is like renting out your stocks with an option to sell at a higher price

- *Covered* means you, the investor, own the stock

- Gives someone an option to *call* (buy) your stock from you at a higher price *(strike price)* than you paid for it

- Option contracts are sold per 100 shares for a *premium* of cash, which adds to your return on the stock. Premiums are deposited on the next business day after the sale of the option

- Example:
  Buy 100 shares IBM @ $83.85 = $8,385 (Price as of July 2004)
  Dividend paid = $/2
  Sell call for January of 2005 @ $95 strike price

- Premium received = $125 (or $250 if option is sold twice in one year and the stock is approximately the same price)

- By third Friday of each month if strike price isn't reached, the option expires and you keep the premium. If the strike price is reached, you sell and make the profit

- If the option is sold twice in one year for approximately the same premium and the stock is not called away (sold), the return is 3%

- If the option is sold twice in one year for approximately the same premium and the stock is called away (sold) at $95, the called return is 17.13%

Claire

In 1970 when I was fourteen years old, I was very lucky to inherit a portfolio of stocks from my grandfather. The portfolio was under my name and my mother's name. My mother has always been very savvy in the stock market, and her financial adviser, Mr. Smith, assumed responsibility for both my sister's portfolio and mine.

My sister and I had identical portfolios. If the adviser suggested buying Pfizer, he bought the same amount of shares for both of us. I would receive dividend checks from time to time, but the majority of those were reinvested in my account. I never paid much attention to my portfolio. Once or twice, my mom sat down with me and tried to describe what the monthly statements meant. I had no idea what she was telling me; the whole financial thing was not something which interested me.

After I graduated from college, my mother decided it was time for both my sister and me to have our accounts in our own names. When the statements came to me, I would briefly look at them and file them away. My sister and I were buying and selling exactly the same things because our adviser was watching over our investments.

When I finished graduate school with a master's in education, I took a job at a small university. It was my first professional job, and I loved working in student affairs. My graduate work had prepared me well, and I was excited about my career. However, I had developed panic attacks and didn't realize what they were. I did not tell anyone about these attacks and never went to a doctor until months later. They became progressively worse.

Around the same time, I met a man named Mark, a financial analyst who was divorced and had a three-year-old boy. Spending time with him seemed to take my mind off the panic attacks, and I could put all my energy into his life. I realize now that I was not at my mental best when I decided to marry Mark. He had joint custody of his son with his ex-wife, and there were ongoing legal issues and expenses.

My portfolio at the time of my marriage to Mark was around $150,000. I had told him about my inheritance before we were married. He had seen a statement laying on the table in my apartment, and I was happy to have him look at it.

Because I had cash on hand, I used it for the down payment on our condo that fall and purchased all the furniture. I figured that I was lucky to have this ready money, and I wanted to share it with my husband. We both would benefit without having to tap into either of our incomes.

After the second year of marriage, Mark approached me about writing a check for $20,000 from my account to place in his account at a discount brokerage house. He wanted to see how well he could invest it for us. The idea seemed reasonable to me, and I trusted him, so I simply pulled out my checkbook and wrote him the check. Looking back at it now, I shudder to think I did such a thing. Of course, I never saw the money again, and to this day I have no idea what happened to it.

Mark then suggested that we put my account in both our names so that we could manage it better. He had me sign a power of attorney form to buy and sell stocks without my prior approval. I thought he would confer with me about his activity and keep me posted. He did, to some degree, at the beginning. However, as my five-year marriage progressed, the portfolio was slowly being gutted.

My husband was working with a stockbroker who noticed how powerful Mark felt with such a portfolio, and this broker seized every opportunity to make trades and commissions on the account. Mark got involved in very speculative trading activities and risky investments. I did not know this until later because I never saw the statements. The statements were mailed to our home, but my work hours were much longer than Mark's, so he always got the mail before I arrived home.

In November 1989 my mother begged me to look at those statements. My father had just passed away, and I was not happy in my marriage. In fact, since 1986 I had been quite depressed, and my work was the only thing that I enjoyed. I was afraid to look at the statements for fear of what I knew I would find.

My mother and I talked about what I would say to Mark so he would not suspect anything. We decided I would say that we were going to inherit some money from my father, and the will required that I review my portfolio before any inheritance could be given. Believe it or not, Mark fell for this story. His greed took over once more.

I remember the day that we sat in the living room, and I reviewed each statement from 1985 to 1989. I went back to 1985 and saw checks written for legal bills, tuition for private school for his son, jewelry that he had bought me, a Rolex that he bought for himself, and many other things. I looked at the statements, but with the amount of trading activity that occurred in one month it was overwhelming. I saw investments made in casinos and other stocks that I could not believe. The account was truly devastated in the crash of October 1987. Of course, that was where the biggest loss occurred, and from that time Mark tried to rebuild it quickly, but of course he couldn't. Basically, the account was down to $15,000.

I was sick. I got a divorce and was in court for two years trying to salvage my money. He fought me tooth and nail about everything. I learned a hard lesson. I had given my husband power of attorney. Each time a question was asked about any investment or about a check that had been written, I had either signed something that I did not look at or understand, or he had purchased stocks without my knowledge. My divorce attorney was excellent, but it became clear in court that my former husband had taken me for most of what I was worth. The judge could even see that, but the money was gone, and technically I had allowed it to happen. I came out of the divorce with $30,000 which came from selling the condo.

My financial adviser was long retired by this time. When he heard what had happened to me, he felt horrible. My sister Lauren had begun working with an associate of his, and so I went to the same adviser, a woman. She knew when she met me what I had been through, and she helped me rebuild my portfolio again, making it a point to educate me as well. It was another hard lesson to learn. I also came to the realization that there are unethical stockbrokers, even in well-established firms. I am very grateful that this financial disaster happened in my early thirties rather than later in my life.

It took me several years to forgive myself for being so naïve and trusting. Fortunately, I found an excellent male therapist who helped me understand on many levels what had happened in my relationship. He reassured me that it was normal to go into marriage trusting your husband, and it was Mark who had violated that trust. He told me to stop beating myself up for past mistakes and helped me become stronger and put my life back on track.

The therapy paid off. When I began to date again, I was better able to speak my truth to potential mates. I would tell them upfront if it wasn't a match, and I felt more in control of my life. Eventually, I met a wonderful man, an established professor on campus, and we began to date. As we became closer, I told him in general terms that I had lost a lot of money in my previous marriage. When he asked me to marry him, I suggested we draw up a **prenuptial agreement** for his protection as well as mine.

It was a hard matter to discuss, as it brought up the issue of trust again. At one point we were going to draft something ourselves, and then we decided it would be better to have an attorney do this. We had to divulge our entire holdings and read through the documents prior to signing. This financial disclosure was actually a great move. We got things out into the open and could freely discuss estate decisions and other issues. By law I was entitled to his pension, a sizeable amount that he had saved over a thirty-three-year period. I suggested that he leave the rest of his assets to his grown children. I had sold my house prior to our marriage and had invested a large sum of money into a major remodel of his house. In the prenuptial agreement, I asked that if the marriage lasted less than five years, I would be reimbursed this amount.

My husband told me that one of the qualities he appreciated the most about me was that I was independent. He knew that he didn't have to worry about me financially, and that freed us both to love one another and enjoy our marriage. By learning from the mistakes of the past and putting my financial investments in order, I gained the confidence to finally attract the right man into my life.

ADVISER'S CORNER

When Claire came to me for investment advice, I knew her trust had been violated and did everything possible to reassure her while working within the framework of her supportive family. I helped her pick new stocks as well as those suggested by her mother and sister.

Claire went back to her practice of saving and reinvesting dividends and profits. She does not spend the principal in her living trust account, continues to work, and funds an IRA every year from her wages. With her prenuptial agreement, she has kept this account separate from her joint assets. She has recouped some of her losses, but still has a port-folio about one-third the value of Lauren's. Confident and happy in her new marriage, she has learned to trust herself and her financial instincts again.

$MART CHOICE

Prenuptial Agreement

- Consult an attorney to draft a *prenuptial agreement,* a legal contract written before marriage which specifies how assets and liabilities would be divided in case of divorce

- If drafted after marriage, the document is called an *antenuptial*

- Frequently executed in remarriage when the couple is older and has more assets

- May protect future earnings and assets as well current ones

- Each person must disclose to the other all financial holdings (bank accounts, investments, properties, etc.)

- Best strategy is for each person to have his or her own outside attorney review the agreement to make sure the document has been drafted correctly and all assets are protected

PAMELA: LADIES OF THE CLUB

"If you have not the experience, ask.
There is no shame in asking, but do not pretend
you know when you don't."

Mother Teresa (1910 – 1997)
Albanian Catholic nun

I came from a well-to-do, conservative family. My father was a very successful commercial building contractor and provided well for his family of five children. I always had everything I needed, although I would have loved to wear those Villager clothes like all the other girls in high school. I first learned about money from my mom who handled the family finances. Every week she sat at the kitchen table and paid the bills and always wrote a check for the church too.

When I was a teenager, I worked in my dad's office to pay for gas for my 1963 Corvair Monza. In college I worked in the dorm. In the summer I worked in a restaurant and retail store to pay my own way for trips to Colorado and California. My brothers took such advantage of my parents that I almost felt obligated to make my own money.

I was married at twenty and found out rather quickly that my new husband had champagne tastes and beer wages. I had a little savings and paid off his bills before we were married, which was a big mistake, because he never did take responsibility for our finances. We lived from month-to-month and always were borrowing $10 from a friend.

After a few years, my friends would laugh at me because I had a spreadsheet for my budget and worked hard to pay something on every account even if it was a mere $5 or $10. It took me two years to pay off the hospital bill for my first child. I didn't like the feeling of not having something in savings. I finally left that schmuck and found a great man.

Bill—I like to call him my Cadillac—was already a successful businessman, another building contractor like my daddy. I had a head for business and was a willing learner and eager participant in our investments. We set our goals right away to buy one piece of property each year and figured when we were ready to retire; we would sell a property a year.

In 1981 we started our own company. We established a credit line with the bank and left good jobs to go it alone. After a few years we wanted to compensate our employees and also establish an IRA program for ourselves, so we opened a **SEP IRA**. The company contributed 7.5%–15% of salaries depending on year-end balances.

In 1996 I was program chairman for a volunteer committee of women at our local art museum. We'd been reading a lot about investment clubs and the Beardstown Ladies, so I invited a stockbroker to speak to our group about creating an investment club. The club was set up under the guidelines proposed by **NAIC** (National Association of Investors Corporation). We started with twenty women each contributing $50 a month.

We research the stocks we are considering, and members take turns presenting the case to buy a particular stock. This allows many of us, who have always depended on our husbands to do the investing, to learn about the stock market, how to choose stocks, and how to invest. Most of us have since opened our own individual accounts. Our adviser came several times and has taught us how to sell covered calls, giving us yet another way to earn money. The group continues to meet and invest each month.

When my parents passed away, I inherited some money which I invested in bonds with staggered maturity dates to provide money as far out as twenty years. Because of my experience in the investment club and the retirement accounts we've set up through our own company, I feel confident in my financial knowledge and more secure in my future.

ADVISER'S CORNER

Pamela's choice of an investment club is a confidence booster— an excellent way to learn the basic skills and language of the investment world. An investment club can be started with a group of novice investors who have relatively little or no experience in investing. NAIC provides educational tools and events to bring the group along and through researching and presenting stocks to the group, every woman becomes the wiser. Other investment clubs are formed by two or more seasoned investors who seed the new club of novice investors and model the invest- ment strategies for the other women.

The important strategy here is to start where you can start with small steps. Practice with $50 a month like Pamela and her friends did, and you will feel comfortable making larger investments when your ini- tial money grows. All the financial education in the world is wasted unless you put it to practical use. Many women find that with the support of other women, they are better able to make that leap of faith into their first investments.

Setting up a SEP IRA was the smartest choice Pamela and Bill could make for their company retirement plan. They can shelter a great deal of money from taxes. They can direct their own investments within the plan. They can retain key employees in their business by sharing this benefit with them.

Pamela and Bill have a college-age daughter who began working in the family business at age sixteen, and they funded a SEP IRA for her as well. Pamela has spent a lot of time sharing her financial knowledge with her daughter, and now the young woman is quite sophisticated about money matters and reads financial education books to increase her understanding of investments.

$MART CHOICES

NAIC

- Join **NAIC** (National Association of Investors Corporation)

- Membership fees for 2005:
  - Individual Stock Membership: $50/year
  - Individual Mutual Fund Membership: $50/year
  - Individual Stock and Mutual Fund Combination Membership: $80/year (best value)

- Read the monthly magazine *(Better Investing Magazine)* for investment tips

- Educational tools and events are available

Four Basic Investment Guidelines:
  - Invest regularly
  - Reinvest all earnings and dividends
  - Buy growth stocks
  - Diversify your investments

- Contact Information:
  - 1-877-275-6242
  - www.better-investing.org

SEP IRA

- **SEP** stands for *Simplified Employee Pension* and is a tax-deferred retirement plan for self-employed individuals

- Simple to set up at a bank, mutual fund company, or brokerage firm

- Funded by the employer (self/company)

- Self-directed investments in stocks, bonds, or cash

- Maximum contribution in 2005: 25% of compensation, not to exceed $42,000

- Must contribute for any employee who has worked three of the five past years at same rate as employer

- 100% vested—always have access to the money under IRA guidelines

- 10% penalty for withdrawals before age 59½

- Required minimum distributions at the age of 70½

GLADYS: BONDING WITH ZEROES

"They talk about a woman's sphere,
As though it had a limit.
There's not a place in earth or heaven.
There's not a task to mankind given
Without a woman in it."

Kate Field (1838 – 1896)
American journalist

My maternal grandparents emigrated from the Netherlands to a Midwest suburb. Grandfather built high-end residences and became wealthy enough to support a household with six children in rather grand style until the Depression wiped out his substantial holdings in the stock market. He was able to recoup to some extent, but the market crash definitely left my mother with a strong instinct to be very careful with money and not to trust that the relative wealth of the moment will last.

This grandfather had a tendency toward exotic spending—a weekly purchase of fresh flowers for his wife, intermittent live-in maids, family trips to Europe (via ship), jewelry, furs, fine furniture and art purchases, a summer home on Lake Michigan, and status cars. None of my mother's siblings completed college, but she and her sisters all married professional men who provided their families with a solid upper-middle-class lifestyle.

Women were supposed to be the protectors of the wealth and run frugal households, watching for the best prices on food, clothing, and gasoline. They were expected to be self-sufficient: to knit and sew for the family, to pay cash and never use a credit card, and to do most home maintenance and cleaning themselves rather than hiring help. The family rarely ate out—meals were home cooked, and on the occasional trip away, we stayed at the least expensive hotels.

All this discipline of being frugal paid off when I met my husband-to-be, Alan, who came from a lower-middle class family. When we married, we blended the most conservative money habits of both families. We drove an eight-year-old vehicle given to us by our parents until we could afford to pay cash for our first car, a $2,000 Dodge Dart. We found an apartment in an old house for only $80 a month and furnished it with hand-me-downs from various family members. My $1,200-per-year scholarship for each of two years of graduate school supplemented the money we earned at summer jobs and allowed us to finish nine years of graduate school, medical school, and residency debt free. Home haircuts, homemade clothes, and riding bicycles to work and school helped us keep our expenses down.

Six years into our marriage when I was earning a salary as a hospital social worker and Alan was being paid as an orthopedic resident, we had our first money outside of living expenses that we could invest. That's when we learned our first hard lesson about money—we followed the advice of a good friend who was a day trader and let him invest $10,000 in ventures of his choosing. While not the Great Depression, we were investing in a recession period, and we essentially lost every penny. Since we went into this investment with the understanding that it was money we could live without, it was not totally devastating, but the experience instilled in us greater caution and conservatism for the future, as well as some reluctance to use friends as advisers.

After two years of military service and slightly over a year in an orthopedic practice that provided only a marginal income, we moved to another part of the state. Alan established his own medical practice, and this thriving business provided us with the first real opportunity to do something with discretionary money. We had built our lakefront home and bought two new cars. The decision to become parents and the subsequent birth of children necessitated a new kind of financial planning.

Diversification of investments became our guiding principle and remains so to this day. We use the services of three financial advisers with different institutions, and only one of them is a friend. We have titled many assets in the name of our family trust to protect them for our children and grandchildren. I have become actively involved in choosing our investments, although initially I was reluctant to do so. I am glad that I have taken the time to educate myself for I have benefited from the practice and fully understand my family's holdings.

Alan and I invested in **zero coupon municipal bonds** to produce income at the time when our children would be needing money for college and Alan might be slowing down his medical practice. One of our financial advisers remained vigilant in searching for these bonds and planned them so that they would mature over the years when we anticipated the greatest college expenses.

I have been blessed with money but have never forgotten my earlier training to be frugal, live within my means, and not try to impress others with what I have. These core values have allowed me to build my wealth slowly and solidly over time and to give back to my family and community.

ADVISER'S CORNER

Gladys is a retired social worker and the wife of a physician. She had her two children when she was in her forties and stayed home to raise them. She and her husband have shared conservative money management philosophies. They avoided debt, paid cash for big-ticket items and lived within their means, whatever their means at a given point in time.

Her investments in the past twenty years have been primarily in zero coupon municipal bonds as well as in a few utility stocks. Her portfolio remained unscathed throughout the stock market crashes and has increased to lofty levels. For many years she relied on her husband to select the bonds but became more involved in choosing the investments. The zero-coupon bonds were designed to provide college funding and to be an accessory retirement vehicle. Gladys now feels so comfortable with investing, she also manages her mother's assets.

$MART CHOICE

Zero Coupon Municipal Bonds

- Tax-free bonds which pay no interest but grow from a smaller amount to a larger amount in a stated period of time

- Long-term and short-term bonds for purchase

- Many maturity dates available

- Great investment tool for college savings or retirement savings

- Highest quality rating is AAA, and these are often insured

- Lower-rated bonds will usually have higher yields to maturity (YTM)

- Purchased in multiples of 5 or 5 face amount, ex: 5M (or $5,000 face amount), not 2, 4, etc.

- Bought at a deep discount and mature at $1,000 per bond
  - e.g. Volusia County Florida, matures 12-1-2019, rated AAA, price $515.47 per $1,000; YTM is 4.421% (price as of September 2004)
  - Investment of $5,154.70 will grow to $10,000 at maturity

- If purchased in the state of residence are completely tax-free—federal, state, local

ANNA AND JENNIFER: MOTHER AND DAUGHTER DUO

*"We must hear the voices and have the dreams of those
who came before us, and we must keep them with us in
a very real sense. This will keep us centered. This will help
us to maintain our understanding of the job we must do."*

*Sonia Sanchez (1934 –)
American essayist, playwright, and poet*

Anna: Forks in the Road

Raised in the Great Depression, I never forgot the lessons of the times to be grateful and mindful of money. A penny was a precious gift. Our maternal grandfather would give each of us a penny when he received his monthly pension check. He would then walk with us to the general store in the neighborhood where we could spend it as we wished. To this day I continue to cherish that copper coin and never hesitate to pick one up when I find it.

My father was innovative in providing for our family. In addition to his work at a local furniture plant, he grew vegetables in his summer gardens, enough so that the surplus could be taken to the farmers' market twice weekly. Mother, a financial wizard, would always find an extra nickel for us to take to Sunday school and to midweek Bible class.

When mature enough, each child was expected to contribute to the welfare of the family—the girls had in-house duties, the boys, outside chores. No one expected an allowance. During the teen years we found neighborhood jobs. The money earned from these jobs was saved or spent as we desired. We were encouraged to save and not spend foolishly, but the final decision was ours. Since instant gratification was not valued in our family, I saved the money earned, which enabled me to purchase a new Easter outfit or a winter coat.

Mother died unexpectedly at age forty-one, and this affected our entire family. My oldest sister inherited the role of money manager and accepted the household responsibilities mother had always performed. Even with my sister at the helm, my mother's absence during high school was a tremendous loss for me.

After graduation in 1943, I attended a Midwestern university to become a teacher. I had a scholarship but had to provide my own room and board. I worked part-time in a senior citizens' home to cover these expenses and still had plenty of leisure time for study and relaxation. After a year of that I wanted to have more of a campus life, so I found a job in the university's cafeteria.

These were the days of World War II, and all of the dorms had been taken over by service men in the V-12 program who were attending the university to become officers in the United States Navy and the Marines. All other students were required to live in approved off-campus housing. I now lived with four other coeds which was more enjoyable but also a lot more expensive. To do this I had to set up a budget for the very first time.

Since there was a serious shortage of teachers, I was part of a group of women in the fast lane and attended classes without a break from June 1943 to September 1944. This enabled me to complete two years of study and qualified me to teach with a special certificate.

My first teaching position was in a one-room country schoolhouse, kindergarten through grade eight. Fortunately I had only fifteen students and not all the grades. The salary for my first year was $1,300 which was typical for that time and no big concern for me. I loved teaching, and being paid for it was inspiration enough to complete my teaching degree. I continued teaching and attending university classes for two more years. At the same time I met my husband-to-be, and we married. My little country school added a second teacher, and it was delightful having a teaching companion. The following year I did not teach due to the birth of our daughter.

When I did return to my profession, it was an easy transition because I had sisters who were eager to baby-sit. I was offered a position at a three-teacher school closer to the city, which meant I needed to learn how to drive and purchase a car to drive to work. During that time I returned to the university for the summers and also took extension classes during the school year. My bachelor of science degree was the first and only degree earned by any of our siblings. I taught for several years in the school system from which I graduated and then in the city schools where I remained for the rest of my teaching career. Throughout my 42 years of teaching, I participated in the **403B plan** offered by my school system. I felt great peace of mind knowing that my retirement account was building as I was making other investments.

After the war, times became easier for my husband, daughter, and me, but salaries remained low. We were savers, and in 1950 were able to build our first home. After living there for seven years, we were able to upgrade to a larger ranch-style home. With two incomes we were able to afford a few extras such as a power boat, yet saving money remained a priority. Both my husband and I were taking extension classes, and I eventually earned my master's degree. This was money well spent. Later, the board of education, to encourage teachers to improve their skills, paid for classes which would meet these criteria. I took advantage of this opportunity and earned an extra thirty hours in education.

Because we continued to save, we were able to purchase eighty acres of riverfront property with a small cabin. We enjoyed this vacation property very much and replaced the cabin with a larger, more comfortable home. After my husband's death, my daughter and I continued to use the home until it became a burden to maintain. At the time we listed it with a real-estate agent, its value had increased considerably. Even though we were sad to give it up, the financial gain consoled us.

It was during this same period we were introduced to the

value of investing in treasury bonds. My husband's mother, a spunky, smart widow who ran her own insurance agency, told us about them. This first paper investment other than the usual bank account ushered us into the realm of stock purchases. We bought shares in a utility and also began to purchase certificates of deposit. Eventually we were introduced to a female adviser at a major brokerage house who became our reliable and trusted consultant.

Each person faces forks in life's road. Making the right choices takes skill and sound financial advice. My family's influence was instrumental in the forks I took. To this day I have a budget and a conscience that do not permit me to stray from the goals I set for myself.

ADVISER'S CORNER

Anna and her husband came to see me when I first became a financial adviser. They opened a joint account with me, and later, her daughter Jennifer opened an account for herself. Both mother and daughter were school teachers and participated fully in the 403B plans offered by the school systems.

Anna built a portfolio of laddered municipal bonds during the 1980s and '90s and continues this type of investing into this decade as her bonds mature. Laddered bonds mean the bonds are staggered to mature (or come due) in different years. This is a smart way to protect your investments against the fluctuation of rising and declining interest rates. Generally, if interest rates go down, bond prices go up and vice-a-versa. The bonds themselves have fixed interest rates which give the investor a more consistent return on her investment over time.

Since Anna's net worth was rising above the estate-tax exemption mark, we set up a life insurance policy to pay estate taxes when Anna dies. Anna is the insured, and Jennifer is the owner and beneficiary of the insurance policy.

She has also invested in utility stocks and real estate investment trusts commonly called REITS. These trusts, like bonds, are a more stable investment and typically pay high interest rates.

$MART CHOICES

403B Plan

- Voluntary retirement plan offered by non-profit organizations such as schools, to which employees may contribute a percentage of their pre-tax earnings

- Employer may match contributions

- Money grows tax-deferred

- Maximum contribution for 2005 is $14,000 for those under age 50 or $18,000 for those over 50

- Several choices of investments—stocks, bonds, cash

REITS

- REIT stands for *Real Estate Investment Trusts*

- The trust owns several properties (usually commercial, but may be residential)

- Usually pay monthly or quarterly income to investor

- Shares traded on a stock exchange

- Share prices not necessarily correlated to stock indices (such as Standard and Poors 500)

- Can own office buildings, apartment buildings, shopping malls and assisted living centers, or homes

- e.g. Senior Housing (SNH is the stock symbol)
  - Owns assisted living centers
  - Share price has been between $13.50 and $20.05 the last 52 weeks
  - Current share price is $17.72
  - Current yield is 7.0% (September 2004)

Jennifer: Let the Buyer Beware

As a Baby Boomer born in 1947, I always felt I had the best of both worlds—the conservativism of my parents and the hope and inspiration of the '60s. My parents helped me to form discipline with money so there would be more than enough for later years. They encouraged me to face my own challenging forks in the road and make the choices that would insure my wealth. My generation taught me it was just as important to align my money with soul as to invest in those things that had meaning for my life.

Mother and I make a good team because our values are compatible. We prefer conservative investments. If a stock purchase does not perform to our expectations, we sell it, take a loss, and reduce the taxes due on the gains of other stocks. While others were caught up in what Alan Greenspan called the "irrational exuberance" of the '90s, I was not tempted to invest in the get-rich-quick opportunities, but kept my eyes firmly fixed on long-term goals. This created awareness to become even more involved in the status of my portfolio and pursue strategies to protect and improve the bottom line. Even so, I was not inclined to invest in high-risk stocks.

As a young adult, I primarily invested in my 403B plan. Like my mother, I became a teacher and took full advantage of my school's retirement plan as this was an opportunity to save in a tax-deferred investment. Later, when my investments grew, I opened an account at a major brokerage house. My adviser was totally on board with my investment strategy and kept me in conservative investments. Working with professionals brought me into contact with other so-called good deals offered at various seminars. That's when I appreciated my father's advice to always weigh the risk against the return.

I received an invitation to a seminar regarding a money-making investment in dairy cows. My father was skeptical but encouraged me to attend nonetheless. Thus, I duly entered "cow seminar" on my calendar.

When the date of the event arrived, I drove to the location, found the room, and chose a seat not far from the speaker. Other curious investors were already there. The speaker explained that each investor would be required to purchase a certain number of cows. The herd would be managed in one central location. The profit from the milk sold would be distributed according to the value of each person's investment. Of course, the expenses would be deducted before the checks went out. It all sounded simple until the question-and-answer period.

I asked the most questions. What happened if a cow became ill or stopped producing milk? What happened if I wanted out of the investment? Who would buy my cows then? Who would determine the value of my cows at that date? If a cow had a calf, who would determine the ownership of that calf and its value? The speaker seemed stumped and couldn't really give me any solid answers.

Not knowing anything about cows—and apparently the broker didn't either—I began to wake up to the idea that this was likely a brainless bovine scam designed to bamboozle the audience. As I listened further, I imagined twenty-five to fifty cows corralled in my parents' back yard because the operation had gone belly up, and I could hardly stop myself from laughing.

My father was relieved to learn that I did not commit any money to this grand opportunity. Over the years, I have recalled this adventure every time I read or hear about another get-rich offer which ultimately folded and left the investor with no recourse. This experience installed a neon BUYER-BEWARE sign in my brain and reinforced the desire to follow the conservative money values I learned from my parents.

Throughout my life I have done very well with my investments. I continued to invest in my 403B for retirement. I purchased long-term care insurance and placed all my assets in a living trust. I made accelerated payments on my home and owned it outright after just a few years. I inherited money from my paternal grandmother and added that to my portfolio. And then, I decided to accept my school system's early-retirement incentive and added that cash to my holdings as well.

When this life change occurred, Mother asked me if I might want to sell my home and share her new condo. We thought long and hard about too much togetherness, but after discussing our concerns and conditions openly, we decided to do it. We are now in the enviable position of being retired with lots of time and cash on our hands and the freedom to travel, attend symphony concerts, and visit our friends. It is truly a charmed life, one we earned slowly and preciously over time.

What warms my soul now is making contributions to my church and other charitable organizations. I tithe regularly. I give annual gifts to our symphony orchestra and local public library system. I support PBS (Public Broadcasting System) and also the university from which I graduated. One of my highest priorities is giving money for children's basic needs through the United Way. It is my way of staying connected to the world's children. These organizations are all deserving causes, and it brings me such joy to participate in their well-being.

ADVISER'S CORNER

It is rare that I have to encourage clients to live a little and spend more of their money, but this is the case with Anna and Jennifer. They have been so conscientious in their investing, so generous in their giving, they deserve to enjoy their wealth even more.

Jennifer's cow story reminds me of several get-rich quick schemes that clients have brought to me over the years, and I have advised to stay away from them all. The surest way to acquire wealth is saving over time in diversified investments, but that is not to discourage those investors who may be starting late. A few well-placed smart choices can give any woman a bump up the wealth ladder.

\$MART CHOICE

Avoiding Investment Scams

- Trust your intuition on high-risk investments that appear too good to be true

- Beware of up-front cash investment; be prepared to lose all.

- Types: some home-based, Internet, and multi-level businesses, certain vacation time share, agricultural, and commodities investments

- Red flags are vague details, marketing plans you don't understand, pie-in-the-sky returns, no clear exit strategy, penalties (stated or unstated) for leaving the investment, free stock, high-pressured close, etc.

- Contact *Better Business Bureau* in your area for brochures on illegal income scams or pyramid schemes plus background checks on companies

- Have outside third party (financial adviser, accountant, and/or attorney) review potential investment

DOROTHY:
TWENTY-TWO HITS AND A MISS

*"Working hard overcomes a lot of other obstacles. You can have
unbelievable intelligence; you can have connections; you can have
opportunities fall out of the sky. But in the end, hard work is
the true, enduring characteristic of successful people."*

Rear Admiral Marsha Evans (1947 –)
US Navy (Retired)
President and CEO of the American Red Cross

It was lunchtime on a day in October 1945, in the Robert
Brooks Projects in Chicago, Illinois. The doctor said, "It's a boy!" The
scream and the kick that followed enabled him to see that he was
wrong. I am a girl; but after twenty-two boys, one could see how he
could make the mistake. I, Dorothy, am the twenty-third child born
to African-American parents Ruth and Johnny Ronny. All of us were
born at home because it was cleaner than the hospital for "Negroes."
By my birth the doctor had replaced the midwife.

It had been a difficult pregnancy for my mother. In fact, the
doctor had suggested to my father that the pregnancy be terminated
because my mother had a weak heart and her life would be threat-

ened, particularly at delivery. My father wanted to follow the doctor's suggestion, but my mother and grandmother, devout Catholics, said, "God would decide; it was not man's decision." On that sunny, warm October day, my mother and I lived, but my fraternal twin died at birth. I would not learn of this until many years later. As my father would often say, "Some things you just don't talk about…you just live with it."

I lived at a time when people in the neighborhood seldom ventured outside the fifteen-block radius they called the 'hood. I never imagined that eventually I would not only leave the neighborhood but would travel internationally and be just as comfortable in the board rooms of Fortune 500 companies as I was in my early years playing in the sandbox outside the Chicago projects.

What changed my life? Some might say it was the education I received from public and Catholic institutions courtesy of hard work, scholarships, and fellowships. Others might say it was an intact family support system of parents, siblings, and my grandmother who cared for me. But mostly, it was the encouragement of my mother and my college mentor who could see possibilities when others were blinded by racial barriers, gender stereotypes, and poverty of aspirations.

I grew up like my brothers. I played baseball, football, and all the other sports boys played—until age twelve when my father told me that I was a girl and should concentrate on cleaning the house, ironing clothes, and becoming a good cook. I couldn't accept this, especially since my father had taught my mother to cook, and he was still a better cook than she. I loved to read and read everything that I could see—books, signs, labels, everything. I read and I questioned so much that by the time I was in third grade, the nuns asked my parents to take me out of Catholic school because my questions were too disturbing for the other students. My father was not pleased, but my mother said, "Perhaps this is God's plan for her."

I enrolled in public school, and at the first conference my teacher informed my parents that I was being promoted to the next grade since I already knew the third-grade curriculum. This happened twice in elementary school, so I entered high school at age twelve and was very immature even at that age. I was still playing with paper dolls.

By then we no longer lived in the projects. We had been forced to move since my father was making $1 an hour and my mother also worked. It didn't matter that they had twenty-three children and three adults, including my grandmother, to feed. Further complicating the move were the restrictive covenants in most deeds which prohibited the sale of property to "Negroes." My father's boss arranged for another employee who was moving out of state to sell his property to my father. The company's attorney removed the restrictive covenant prior to the transfer of the property. My father was a hard worker, and his boss wanted him to be able to concentrate on work, not take time off to look for a place to live.

Initially, I was sent to a vocational school because most counselors thought Negroes should learn a trade. My mother protested, and after a review of my test scores, I was transferred to a high school that served as a feeder school for the University of Chicago. I was placed in accelerated classes. Now my questions were encouraged, and they began to open up a new life for me.

My father was a very traditional black man. When I earned a scholarship to a university, he wanted to know if he could sell it—feeding twenty-three kids was not easy—or transfer it to one of the boys. After all if a girl were too educated, she would have difficulty getting a husband. I didn't believe this because my mother was a licensed practical nurse, and my father who left school after sixth grade had married her. My mother prevailed. I was off to the university at age sixteen.

It was the first time I had been away from home alone overnight. The university was only sixty-five miles away but it was a world away from where I grew up. The scholarship covered only tuition and books, so I cleaned houses and worked on the switchboard at the dormitory to pay for housing and food.

I was pretty naïve about racism at the university, but when I was denied placement in Honors English and graded down on some of my papers, I decided to make an appointment with the dean of women. I explained that my English teacher was giving A's to all the papers I wrote for other people but not to those I wrote for myself. I didn't know then that I was not allowed to sell papers. The bookstore sold condensed papers, so I thought I could sell mine. I needed money, and I loved to write.

The dean said she wanted me to write a set of papers one more time. I was to bring all of them to her and tell her which one I would be turning in as my own. I did that after she assured me that my customers would have immunity if they ceased purchasing papers with this final transaction. She agreed that I was keeping the best paper. As in the past, all my clients got an A, and I received a C+.

The dean had a talk with my professor. I never knew what she said to him, but I received an A in English and was placed in Honors English during the next term. I remember that day better than yesterday. I had found both a friend and mentor willing to take a stand for my education.

In my junior year my mother had a stroke, and I left the university. Before I departed, I went to see the dean of women to thank her for all she had done for me and to tell her that I wouldn't be back the next semester. The money I had saved would be needed at home. The dean wrote a check for my tuition. When I protested that I didn't know when I would be able to pay her back, she said, "Don't pay it back to me. Do something for someone else." Here she was helping me again. I have never forgotten my gratitude for her generosity that enabled me to return for my senior year and graduate.

After college, I applied for various teaching positions in the Chicago area. During those days photographs were placed on one's credentials before they were sent out to prospective employers. I was at home with my mother, so my credentials went out without my picture. I received many offers, but I accepted the one from a superintendent who called me, interviewed me by telephone, and offered me the job. It was in a suburb of Chicago, a place which I later learned had no blacks, Catholics, or Jewish people. I was a black Catholic, and my presence would definitely shake things up.

I had been hired to teach fifth grade and to develop a special education and reading program for elementary and junior high students. At twenty, I didn't drive, so I had my new husband drive me to the school-district office and wait in the car until I had met briefly with the superintendent and completed the employment papers.

When I entered the office, the receptionist remained seated and asked, "Do you need something?" Her tone sounded more like, "I know you are not enrolling your child here." I told her, "I am Mrs. Smith, the new teacher, and I have an appointment with the superintendent." She got up, ran to the superintendent's secretary, and spoke to her as though I were not in the room. The superintendent's secretary ran into his office and spoke to him as though the door were not open. He came out, ushered me into his office, and closed the door and the blinds which covered windows with a view of the quiet side street. I was not to be seen by outside parties who might happen by on this beautiful, sunny summer afternoon.

He turned to me without offering a seat and asked if I had noticed how the neighborhood had changed on my way from the city. I knew what he meant, but I took a seat and responded, "Yes, it was industrial, and it became very residential." He said, "That is not what I meant. You see, we have never even hired a Negro maintenance man before." I told him that I didn't think that he was going to pay me all that money to be a maintenance person because obviously, I was not a man. He said, "How would you feel if you went into the teachers' lounge, and no one spoke to you?" I told him that I would be quite relieved because I was quite particular about whom I spoke to. He laughed and said that he was going to pay me $500 more a year for combat pay and that my presence would help solve another problem the district was having with the Equal Employment Opportunity people. I was glad that I had kept my cool and allowed laughter to diffuse the tension of the moment. As I left that afternoon, I couldn't help but think what a blessing it had been that my photograph never appeared on my résumé, or they would have screened me out of many segregated school districts.

When I started my job, I went to the teachers' lounge every day. I would smile each time a new teacher would enter, and then I'd return to my book. After a few weeks they were short a fourth at bridge and asked me if I played. When I said yes, it was another step toward integration.

After two-and-a-half years of wonderful teaching, I gave notice to the district. Everyone, even the receptionist, said, "Don't go; you really made a difference here. We will miss you." I asked them to give me one gift, to extend that same tolerance and welcome to the next person of different race or religion—black, Catholic, or Jew—who came into their district. They agreed they would.

Over the years, I taught preschool through graduate school, including every area of special education except the deaf and hearing-impaired. I went back to school to pursue **advanced degrees** and eventually obtained my doctorate in human development. I had a private psychological counseling practice for ten years, was a dean at a state university, and lectured and taught at many other universities. I also served as a government appointee for three governors and held elected office as well.

One morning, after a life-changing experience, I decided to leave all the structure. I wanted to travel and consult when it was convenient. The timing was right, and the consulting jobs were plentiful. To reduce my expenses, I incorporated my own travel agency. I kept this agency for twenty-two years. I had my TIAA-CREF retirement account, some real estate investments, and my savings.

After 9/11 everything changed in travel and consulting as companies cut many services, expenses, and trips. My daughter, who had by then earned her doctoral degree, had three children in school and a newborn. She was on tenure track at a university and in the middle of an important research project. Her husband traveled a great deal, and she needed a nanny. I established a **virtual office** for my travel agency and my consulting business. Then I became the nanny-granny. My grandmother had cared for me while my mother worked. Now it was my turn to help my grandchildren.

It was the perfect time to go virtual with my business. The tools of my trade were simply a cell phone, laptop computer with the requisite software, a website, and an e-mail address. Customers made specific travel requests on the telephone or by e-mail, and I booked the trips, hotels, and cars for them. I reduced overhead because I no longer had to pay for physical office space, a secretary/inside agent, and other related costs such as utilities and insurance. I saved a tremendous amount of time by no longer dealing with the anonymous shoppers who wanted a great deal of information but did not want to book trips. I was free to care for my grandchildren, travel, and still serve my clientele.

My father used to say, "Twenty-two hits and a miss," referring to me as the "miss" among his twenty-three children, but I knew I was special and I was determined to put my talents to good use. My life has been, to a large extent, about giving back God's blessing by "doing something for someone else," as my dean asked me to do. That has been the true richness in my life. I am grateful for the women who believed in me and now for the opportunity to support my own children and grandchildren. That is, after all, the best giving back for all my future generations.

ADVISER'S CORNER

I have always been an advocate of pursuing advanced degrees, as it generally improves one's earning potential and ability to invest. Over the years, we've had dozens of interns at the brokerage firm, and I encouraged them all to enroll in additional certification and training programs such as CFA (Chartered Financial Analyst), which would enable them to become mutual fund managers. My M.A. in education has served me well in teaching seminars to investors.

In the current job market, however, an advanced degree is not an automatic guarantee to a higher salary. We are experiencing both high unemployment and high underemployment, as many people with advanced degrees are earning less than their degree median income. If a working adult has not stayed current in her field, she may need to retrain or recareer into another field at a lower starting wage. Some degrees, such as M.B.A.'s, are almost oversold for the market and may not be necessary or even beneficial for career advancement in some companies. Before you commit to an expensive and extended graduate program, ask your employer or other professionals in the field about the income and advancement potential for that degree.

The beauty of the virtual office is that it can be conducted from home or any other location that is quiet, private and secure. Many working parents (and grandparents like Dorothy) are opting for the virtual office, because it saves them lengthy commutes, gas, and automobile expenses, enhances the quality time they can spend with their families, and increases productivity by streamlining operations. Many companies are finding it is more cost-effective to set up home-based offices than to rent expensive work space in commercial buildings, and they are packaging the virtual office with flex hours and other perks to retain valued employees.

$MART CHOICES

Advanced Degrees

- Take advantage of company's educational benefits to complete an advanced degree

- Apply new skills immediately to demonstrate additional competencies to employer

- Education keeps you current and more attractive to employers

- Explore part-time and distance-learning options to avoid loss of income and career momentum

- Pay as you go versus taking on large student loans

- Consult professionals in field to establish income and promotion benefits of pursuing advanced degrees

- Be realistic about fluctuating job market—higher income and job security are not guaranteed

- **Median 2003 Income by Educational Level***
  - Some high school $20,000/year
  - HS grad/GED: $26,000/year
  - Associate's Degree: $33,000/year
  - Bachelor's Degree: $43,000/year
  - Master's Degree: $53,000/year
  - Professional: $81,000/year
  - Doctorate: $70,000/year

- Pay varies according to degree and geographical area (teachers may start at $36,000/year with a bachelor's degree vs. a computer programmer who may start at $61,000/year)
  *www.salary.com

Virtual Office

- Costs to set up and operate (2005)
  - $1,500 laptop (one-time purchase)
  - $100 cell phone purchase + $50/ monthly usage fees
  - $150 website development (+ upgrades as needed)
  - $25 travel software/monthly
  - $27 Internet fee/monthly
  - $195 errors and omissions insurance annually (protects service-oriented businesses from legal actions due to errors and omissions in scheduling and implementing services)

- Benefits include:
  - Flexible work hours
  - Home-based environment
  - Reduced overhead
  - Ease of marketing services

JOY: DARE TO DREAM

*"I've always believed that one woman's success
can only help another woman's success."*

*Gloria Vanderbilt (1924 –)
American fashion designer*

I was eleven years old when my mother's dream came true.
From her, I learned that perseverance is necessary in attaining precious goals.

My mother and father were tenant farmers who were very
poor. They worked a rental farm and were required to pay 50% of
their earnings to the landlord. All six of us children were born and
raised on that farm, and mother wanted more for us.

After twenty years of subservience, my mother, as keeper of
the purse, dreamed of buying a farm of her very own. With $1 she
opened a bank account to which she added every possible dollar she
could squeeze from their meager earnings. Eventually she had saved
enough for a down payment and bought a farm on a land contract.

I worked our family farm for several years and when I graduated from high school, I had some goals of my own. Attending college was financially impossible, so I found a job in a local factory and
began saving from my weekly paycheck. I met my husband-to-be,

Clark, and we married when I was just nineteen. We newlyweds had barely set up house when Clark was drafted into the army and sent to Korea. We were apart for two years.

To save money, I left our apartment and moved back home with my parents. Mother would not accept room and board from me knowing that the money I saved would be put to good use. I still had my job and paid my own bills and car payment and managed to save $1,000 from my wages. Clark also sent his allotment checks home, and I put them directly into our savings.

With his tour of duty completed, Clark returned home and was very pleased that I had saved a nest egg for us. We bought our first home with a $1,000 down payment on a land contract for $5,000. House payments during the 1950s were $35 per month.

Clark was now employed at an insurance company and participated in the company retirement plan. When our children were born, I chose to stay home and care for them but did not sacrifice my financial goals. I provided day care in our home to supplement Clark's income and continued to save. Eventually, I returned to work and participated in my company's saving plan as well.

As our children grew, so did their needs. We had set aside some college savings for them but also asked them to contribute. They earned good grades in school, worked, and got scholarships, which provided for most of their education.

When we retired, we each had pension funds with our companies, and we decided to roll them over into an **IRA rollover**. This allowed us to streamline our retirement savings into one account.

In the mid-1980s Clark became ill with lung cancer, and he wanted to make sure that I understood our family finances and could manage our portfolio when he died. He reviewed our budget system and investments, and we both went to appointments with our financial adviser. I was already familiar with our retirement plans. Having this information gave me great peace of mind.

No woman ever knows how her life will evolve. Like the river, there have been many turns in my journey. Clark died and some time later, I found love again. My husband and I live a simple, contented life. We enjoy traveling and spending time with our family. I think my mother would have been pleased. It was she, more than anyone else, who taught me to follow my dreams.

ADVISER'S CORNER

It was a smart move for Joy and her husband to review finances together before his death. Many women are absolutely panicked by a sudden death or divorce and ill-prepared to take over the family's financial reins. When Joy was first widowed, she still possessed substantial assets in her home and her IRA rollover and had a detailed understanding of the big financial picture. Now seventy-two, she takes minimum distributions from her IRA. She and her new husband both receive Social Security benefits, and the combined income allows them to live comfortably.

 # $MART CHOICE

IRA Rollover

- IRA rollover allows investor to transfer assets from a qualified plan such as a 401K or 403B to an individual IRA and pay no tax at the time

- Directly transferred from employer's plan to a financial institution such as a bank or brokerage

- No tax until withdrawn

- Must start partial withdrawals by age 70½

- Self-directed investments in stocks, bonds, and cash

ANNETTE: THE CZ GIRL

"Woman must not accept; she must challenge.
She must not be awed by that which has been built up around her;
she must reverence that within her which struggles for expression."

Margaret Sanger (1883 – 1966)
Nurse, activist, and founder of Planned Parenthood

Both of my grandfathers helped build the Panama Canal. One grandfather was the secretary to Colonel Gorgas. He worked with Gorgas to control malaria and yellow fever so people could live to build the canal. He was a brilliant mechanic, as was my father. The other grandfather worked with the railroads that were so important in the building of the canal.

I was born in Panama, Canal Zone, to parents who had grown up in the Zone. All of us children who grew up there were known as CZ brats because we had so much. We had great after-school sports, dances, and many community-sponsored events. I don't remember any crime, and we could go anywhere by ourselves. There weren't many cars, so we walked and biked double and did almost anything as long as we followed our curfew. We had to be home when the streetlights came on and the DDT truck came through spewing mosquito killer

It was a fun and independent childhood. Every other year we came to the States for three months on Canal Zone ships. Passage for employees was free. I attended school in New York for those three months. The Canal Zone schools were much harder. In the CZ there was no television, so I was always organizing something—writing and distributing neighborhood newspapers, organizing fund-raisers for some great cause, or putting on talent shows and dance shows with my friends. We always charged admission but not enough to keep people away. One or two pennies were fine, and we would give all the proceeds to our causes. Money was no problem; of course, movies were just a nickel then, as were candy bars and gum. We had few needs and nothing to spend money on until we went to the United States.

When I was nine years old, I boarded a train to travel to the interior of Panama for a weekend ranch party with my friends. Coming back I fell asleep, and the porter who was supposed to be watching over me didn't watch. Awakening when the train stopped at the last station, I got off the train amidst crowds of very colorful people in turbans and other non-European clothes. Aware that I was not on the fifty-mile Canal Zone strip but had landed in a major city outside the United States jurisdiction, I searched for a friendly taxi driver and asked to be driven to the Canal Zone please. We always had to say *please* and *thank you*. When we miraculously arrived in front of my house inside the protected zone, I told him I would be right back with his money. Taking my dependable piggy bank, I shook out the fare and paid him.

No one was home. My parents and sisters, in a panic, searched for me while I was calmly searching for my dependable piggy bank. I doubt I tipped the driver, but he thanked me and went on. I was confident and lucky to have had such a positive interaction in such a sticky situation. My parents arrived soon after, and I was surprised to see them so worried and upset. Remembering their reactions tempered my future decisions about traveling to seamy spots. I still went; I was just careful. My two sisters and I, along with my parents, left Panama for the Midwest when I was thirteen.

Neither of my parents had a college education. My father was trained for his leadership role on the Canal through lengthy, rigorous apprenticeships. Through him I gained the value of learning by doing and appreciated the nursing training I received at a major Midwestern university. In the late 1950s we nursing students provided a service for our local hospital, and in turn, received free room and board and learned a tremendous amount. I appreciated putting in my time, and even volunteered as a candy striper, where I soon discovered I was a glutton for punishment.

My marriage to a medical student produced two beautiful children, but we later divorced and I moved to another city. There I worked at a children's hospital and went to a local university for what I call my top-notch "union cards": my M.S. in nursing and a Ph.D. in educational sociology. These union cards helped me get good seats in restaurants, a little more attention on the phone, and other useful perks. During my doctoral work I married my second husband, and we merged two families that included five children. That was a real test of management skills and self-control.

Still in love with tropical areas, I chose Hawaii for our honeymoon. Once there, we purchased volcanic land for $19,000. At that time this could be equated to buying swamp land in Florida. We paid off the land in about nine years and camped on the island to evaluate whether we should sell or build. We later built a vacation home there with much of our own sweat and ingenuity for about $130,000 and then rented the house for twenty-three years. Because of this ownership, our family took many trips to Hawaii. We worked on the property while there and managed it from the Midwest. We also had a local property manager. The home recently sold for close to $500,000, making our **real estate in a resort area** one of our most lucrative investments.

When faced with a terminally ill husband and a young daughter, I retired abruptly while my nursing career was at its peak. It was the right choice. Our four other children, though young adults, also needed support. As the old song says, you have to "Know When to Hold Them, Know When to Fold Them."

I bought my first stock on the advice of some male friends and had some small success. I began purchasing stocks and selling them when I had realized a $1,000 gain. I quickly learned that I only made money when I sold with a gain. I wished years later I'd kept that knowledge closer to my actions.

The stock market collapse in the 2000s caught me traveling

and not paying attention. My portfolio had dwindled to half its original amount as I watched passively. I realized the importance of investment diversity—real estate, cash, bonds, mutual funds, stocks—as well as diversity in one's life—personal skills, knowledge, support, friends, and family.

After forty-one years of what I call on-duty parenting, I recently enjoyed my last child's graduation from college. I am working for myself, mapping out where, what, how, and with whom I want to live the rest of my life. To manage my equity portfolio, I recently began working with a financial adviser. I am rich in family with five wonderful children, four sons-in-law and one daughter-in-law better than I could have picked. My nine grandchildren are following their parents' plans for them. My worldly possessions far outweigh my current needs. I am thankful to be in this privileged position.

ADVISER'S CORNER

Real estate in resort areas can be an excellent investment if it's located in an area like Hawaii, Florida, or Southern California, with widespread travel appeal and a tropical or temperate climate. The investor must be committed, as Annette and her husband were, to visiting the property regularly, maintaining it, and having it properly managed in the owner's absence. The best way to maximize this investment is to rent it out for the months or weeks the owner will not be using it which more than likely will pay for the taxes, insurance, and yearly upkeep in addition to some of the mortgage payments, if any, on the property. But anticipated rental revenues are not reason alone to purchase a property. The investor must be able to comfortably go it alone or get a group of investors to cover any increased debt and expenses. Otherwise, it could become an expensive cash drain that undermines other investments.

One should also make a distinction between a vacation property and a vacation time share. Many banks will not grant loans for time share properties and there can be many hidden costs and conditions for using and exchanging time shares. So, time shares are definitely buyer-beware investments.

$MART CHOICE

Real Estate in Resort Areas

- Location, location, location

- Often located near water

- Can be used to generate rental income

- In the last five years resort properties on the Kona Coast in Hawaii have appreciated 20.4% per year

- In the last five years properties in San Diego County, California, have appreciated 21% per year
  - The national average is 5.8% per year (*Smart Money* magazine, May 2004)

DOREEN: THE WORLD TRAVELER

"As a woman I have no country. As a woman I want no country. As a woman my country is the whole world."

Virginia Woolf (1882 – 1941)
English author

My husband and I want to die and run out of money at the same time. We decided that we would enjoy our retirement—travel the world and do what we've always wanted to do. We've set up our investments with that in mind.

I was a Depression baby and have always lived very frugally. I basically lived from paycheck to paycheck, not always successfully. Therefore when I had a chance to save in my company's 401K plan, I took advantage of it to the fullest. As a result, I had a large IRA rollover, as did Phil.

We take two-week vacations every summer and spare no expense. We fly first class, stay in the best hotels, and eat most of our meals in fine dining restaurants with superb food and great wine. That's how we savor every moment of our trip. We've traveled extensively in Europe and the Middle East and usually purchase one or two treasures from each destination, along with gifts for others. We always use an **airline credit card** which earns us air miles for all expenses charged on the card.

During our travels in Mexico, we met new friends who have a villa in Puerto Vallarta and a home in Germany. We plan to visit them in Germany this summer and then continue on through several other European countries. The trip will cost approximately $5,000 which we will take out of our $20,000 annual travel allotment. Our invested assets, excluding our house, are almost sufficient to generate enough income to cover travel expenses without dipping into the principal.

We've found that we can still indulge in these trips if we manage our monthly income well and make periodic reviews of our investments with our financial adviser. I keep a binder with a page for each month's expenses. The pension check is deposited at the beginning of the month, and all other expenses are automatically deducted from the checking account. All VISA charge slips are saved, and we set aside cash for these expenses before the bill arrives. We use our Social Security income and any exceptional amounts are taken from the cash-management money-market accounts. Our adviser put us in **laddered bonds** that come due when we need extra cash for a trip.

Having lost my only brother to a heart attack when he was forty-three, I am aware of the brevity of life and live each day to its fullest.

ADVISER'S CORNER

When Doreen and Phil retired, they set up an IRA rollover from 401K plans at their companies. I put them in laddered treasury bonds called TIGRs (Treasury Investment Growth Receipts) coming due when extra cash was needed for a trip. At this point Doreen has begun to use her principal because the lower interest rates on her new bonds do not generate enough income. Both she and Phil have provided for long-term care needs through insurance, and this has been a variable, since premiums have now doubled. They save monthly for long-term care and estimated income taxes using their Social Security income.

$MART CHOICES

Airline Credit Card

- An airline credit card earns you miles for every dollar spent

- Charge major purchases* on it to accumulate miles

- Pay the bill in full at end of each month so no interest is charged

*Some people charge everything on these cards, so they can quickly accumulate free tickets. It's important to be financially responsible with any credit card and only charge what you can pay off in full the next month.

Laddered Bonds

- Bonds that are purchased with laddered (varying) maturities

- Money comes due when needed

- Protect against interest-rate risk

- Can be done with any type of bond—coupon, zero-coupon, corporate, treasury, and municipal bonds

LOUISE: FUNDING COLLEGE

"The future belongs to those who believe in the beauty of their dreams."

Eleanor Roosevelt (1884 – 1962)
First Lady, U.S diplomat, and reformer

You might say I had an idyllic childhood, vacationing at our lakeside cottage every summer. We lived in our bathing suits, swimming three or four times a day and played around in two small rowboats. There was time to make popcorn and fudge, to have hot dog roasts, sing, and pound out music on an old organ. On weekends my dad came up to the lake, and he would thrill us by telling the scariest stories by candlelight and planning treasure hunts for chocolates wrapped in gold foil. Sometimes he would row us through the lake channels to Lakeland, where he bought us sodas or sundaes before rowing home in the dark.

But when I was fifteen, tragedy struck our family as my father was coming home from a business trip. At three in the morning we received a phone call from a reporter asking about my dad. We were devastated to hear that the plane he was in had crashed and all on board had been killed. At the time my mother was visiting a sister in another state, and we had to send her a telegram telling her of the fatal crash. The details were kept from us. The crash was rumored to be sabotage because Dad was working on defense projects, and as a result, all arrangements had to be made through the Canadian Embassy. We were not allowed to read the news stories, and I didn't see them until I went through my mother's papers years later.

Mother sued the airline and got a small settlement for each of the families deprived of a breadwinner. Though she had only a sixth-grade education, she continued to educate herself. Very involved with a Christian children's home, she took special cases into her home. She was very gregarious and traveled cross country. She lived past ninety.

I married after attending but not completing college, and my husband and I had four children. We considered education to be essential and bought a set of encyclopedias for our children before we purchased a television. When I reached the age of fifty-four, I finished college with a bachelor's degree in social work.

I never forgot what it meant to lose someone suddenly, and I think that tragedy influenced me to plan ahead. So, even though I have rather meager assets, I set up **UGMA and UTMA** accounts to help fund college for my grandchildren. I bought mutual funds in these accounts and hope that the ready money will inspire them to finish their education.

Every child deserves a cherished childhood and by contributing to the education of my grandchildren, I am ensuring that my future generations will be well cared for.

ADVISER'S CORNER

The UGMA and UTMA are excellent ways for parents and grandparents to earmark money for education and monitor the savings until the child reaches age of majority. They are simple to set up and have low tax liability since they are taxed at the child's, not the parent's, tax rate, and then only if the earnings exceed a certain amount.

The downside to this investment is that once the child reaches age of majority, the money is legally his or hers and could be spent for uses other than education. All the more reason to instill the value of education at an early age, as Louise and her husband did with their children and grandchildren.

$MART CHOICES

UGMA and UTMA

- Custodial savings accounts set up for minors under the child's social security number

- UGMA stands for *Uniform Gifts to Minors Act*

- UTMA stands for *Uniform Transfers to Minors Act*

- Anyone can be the custodian (parent, grandparent, or another adult) and contribute to the account

- Child controls funds when she or he reaches *age of majority* (18 or 21, depending on the state of residence)

- May be invested in stocks, bonds, and cash

PATRICIA: CLIMBING THE LADDER

"Even a stopped clock is right twice every day. After some years, it can boast of a long series of successes."

Marie Van Ebner-Eschenbach (1830 – 1916)
Australian author

Born in October 1929 during the stock market crash, I was the fifth child of eight with parents who both had college degrees. My father had a B.S. in animal husbandry and ran our thousand-acre working farm, raising grains, feed cattle, and hogs. In fact, he developed a three-way crossbreed of hogs. My mother had graduated from law school in 1922, the only woman in her class. She was the first female lawyer in our state to defend a man for murder, and she won the case.

The 1930s were very tough years for our family—first the Depression and then seven years of drought. We children all attended a one-room school, and I was the only one in my grade for eight years in a row. After high school where I was valedictorian, I went on to college, as did all three of my brothers who were delayed from attending because of the war. I had a scholarship, and they received funds from the G.I. Bill.

After college I taught for a few years and married in 1955. I began tracking my husband's stocks and became interested in the market. Possessing a $1,000 inheritance from my parents, I invested in Westbury Fashions. I lost everything when the company declared bankruptcy. It was a lesson learned in a hurry—investments do not automatically increase in value. As a member of an investment club for a few years, I continued to invest and put all my profits back into the market. Buy and hold was my philosophy. Now, as a senior citizen, I am buying fewer common stocks and have increased fixed-income investments.

My husband, who is eighty-two, is now getting a bit forgetful. He recently came to me on our forty-ninth anniversary and gave me a package, saying, "I'm sorry I'm a day late—yesterday was our fiftieth anniversary." I replied, "No, it was our forty-ninth." He took his gift and left. Guess I'll have to wait until next year—another delayed dividend!

My greatest pleasure these days comes from giving, and it is a joy to put money into the grandchildren's **529 college-saving plans**. When my husband and I die, there will be considerable assets to distribute. Not wanting our grandchildren to be reckless with their money, we felt it was best if we specifically designated these accounts for education.

To match my desire for more fixed-income investments, my adviser suggested **laddered municipal bonds**, which come due at staggered dates and serve as a hedge against fluctuating interest rates. When the bonds mature, I simply reinvest them in more bonds within my portfolio.

Every investor has moments when she thinks she can outsmart an investment, but that earlier lesson with Westbury Fashions taught me to be conservative and build wealth slowly over time.

ADVISER'S CORNER

Many parents and grandparents prefer 529 plans over the UGMA and UTMA, because the money must be used for higher education, and tax-exempt withdrawals can be made from 2002–2010 to pay for college expenses. These accounts are owned by the adult for the benefit of the child and are also transferable to other children. The parents may also use it for their own education. Every state offers some version

of a 529 plan, and the investor is free to invest in plans from other states.
Laddered municipal bonds are a smart choice for Patricia's port-
folio, because they protect against fluctuations in interest rates and
mature tax free.

$MART CHOICES

529 Plan

- Tax-deferred college savings plan run by states and set up with mutual fund companies

- Must be used for higher education

- Can be funded by anyone

- Owned by the adult for the benefit of the child

- Tax-exempt withdrawals from 2002 to 2010 if used to pay education expenses

- Are transferable to other children

- May be invested in a variety of mutual funds designated by the states

- May buy 529 plans from other states

Laddered Municipal Bonds

- Tax-free bonds invested in cities, counties, and states and their respective schools and improvement projects (such as roads and transportation)

- Pay interest semiannually

- Protect against interest rate fluctuations if laddered to mature every year

- Highest quality rating is AAA, and these are often insured

JEAN: THE PITFALL OF PROCRASTINATION

"We are not what we know but what we are willing to learn."

Mary Catherine Bateson (1939 –)
American anthropologist and linguist

When I was about ten, my mother assigned me the task of taking the mortgage payment to the bank. It was $12.50, and she always said, "Don't lose it; it has to be paid today." Having this financial responsibility at a young age influenced me to be careful with money.

In 1947 I left home to be married, determined to save money whenever possible. We moved out of state so my husband could go to school on the G.I. Bill. He worked part-time, and I worked full-time. We didn't have much money. If on a Tuesday we had 17¢ and needed milk and bread, we bought the bread and drank water until payday on Friday.

After my husband graduated, we moved back to the Midwest and were able to save $2 a month. Sadly, my husband died at fifty-five, when I was just fifty and not eligible for Social Security for another ten years.

Later an old friend came back into my life, and we married, keeping our finances separate. My new husband shared that since his first wife's death, he'd been working with a woman adviser who reviewed his investments semi-annually and made recommendations for his portfolio. At one of these reviews, she suggested that we set up a **living trust**, so that if one of us died before the other, we could settle our estate without the hassles of probate.

We discussed this at length and intended to set up the trust when we returned from our winter vacation in Florida. Unfortunately, we never made it. My husband became ill on the trip and died suddenly without the trust in place. Even on the way to the hospital he was saying, "You know, I never made out that trust." He knew he was dying and regretted leaving me with our affairs so unsettled.

At the time of his death we each had grown children and it was quite an involved process settling his estate in probate and distributing his assets to his children. It was expensive, time-consuming, and worst of all, upsetting to all parties concerned. Shortly after he died, I set up my own living trust, so I would spare my children the same hassles.

I had always been taught to be careful with money and felt I should have seen this pitfall coming, but I didn't. Waiting cost us dearly. I caution my children to never put off to tomorrow what they can do today, especially when it involves their money.

ADVISER'S CORNER

As an adviser, I can educate clients, make recommendations, and do my best to protect their principal and assets. In this case, Jean and her husband had good intentions of following through, but tragedy struck before they could implement their plan. The more assets an investor acquires, the greater the need for thorough estate planning.

With a living trust, one must both set up the trust with an attorney and then fund it—that is, re-title the assets in the name of the trust. If the trust remains unfunded, the assets are considered outside of the trust and are therefore not protected by it.

Such was the case with Evelyn, a friend of one of my clients. She was a single, retired woman who owned a lovely condominium and had the foresight to meet with an attorney to set up her trust. However, when

Evelyn died very suddenly at the age of sixty-seven, it was discovered that either through her ignorance or the attorney's negligence, the condominium had not been re-titled in the name of the trust by means of a quit claim deed, and her estate had to pass through probate. This oversight cost her estate, and consequently her heirs, several thousand dollars and several months' delay.

 # $MART CHOICE

Living Trust

- Written agreement that designates who will manage your assets while you are living, or if you should become incapacitated, and when you die

- Revocable, can be changed at any time

- Usually, grantor is trustee while alive

- Grantor appoints successor trustee(s)

- May have co-trustees (ex. husband and wife)

- No probate required if assets are properly funded (re-titled in the name of the trust)

- When properly executed includes:
  - a *will* (often called a *pour-over will*) which pours over an individual's requests regarding asset distribution, etc., into the trust
  - a *durable power of attorney for health care* which designates a spouse or family to be attorney-in-fact and make health care decisions for you should you be incapacitated

- *Probate* is an expensive and time-consuming process of distributing an estate according to wishes expressed in a will

---

GAY: LIVING WHERE
TRUE WEALTH RESIDES

*"My idea of feminism is self-determination,
and it's very open-ended; every woman has the right to
become herself, and do whatever she needs to do."*

Ani DiFranco (1970 –)
American musician and singer

The heart knows nothing of wealth or status. I was the daughter of a wealthy entrepreneur builder in Chicago in the Frank Lloyd Wright era, privy to a privileged lifestyle. I remember growing up with servants in our mansion and taking trips on big steamships to Europe. Yet when it came to love, I married my college professor, a man eight-and-a-half years my senior who made a mere $26,000 a year. I never finished my degree and was content to be a professor's wife, entertaining his colleagues and making a warm, inviting home for him and our children.

When we were first married, my husband managed the finances, and although his salary was meager, we always had more than enough and still managed to save. Years later, he began to teach me about our investments and together we sought the advice of a financial adviser who recommended that we consider **long-term care insurance** to meet elderly health care needs and serve as a safeguard to protect our $200,000 portfolio. By this time, my husband was in his late eighties and the premiums were too expensive for him, but we did take out insurance for me. The premium was $309 per month. We purchased this with the income we made from our bonds and **bond funds.**

After my husband's death at ninety-one, my health began to deteriorate and I made the choice to move to a retirement home. Now I use my interest income from the bonds to pay for my daily living expenses: room and board, newspaper, cable television, and automobile expenses. Any money I have left over, I spend as I see fit.

I have had numerous medical problems but am considered too high-functioning to receive benefits from my long-term care insurance. According to their guidelines, I must be incapable of performing two out of five activities of daily living (such as eating, bathing, dressing, transferring in and out of bed) before they will allow me to draw benefits.

I am now nearly eighty-seven and enjoy living in the retirement home where I can participate in many activities with long-time friends. Like many of the seniors here, I reminisce about my one great love and have missed my husband every day since his death. My true wealth always resided in that love.

ADVISER'S CORNER

Prior to Gay's death last year, her health had deteriorated to the point that she was about to draw on her long-term care insurance and had applied for benefits. If she had needed it, it would have met a good percentage of her health care needs and saved her investment portfolio. The expense of treating a long-term illness can wipe out wealth faster than anything else, so I always recommend this insurance to my clients. It may be used in residential facilities such as assisted living centers and retirement homes and also for in-home health care.

When Gay and her husband first came to me over twenty-five years ago, I wanted to match their need for conservative investments with a bond fund, which is a mutual fund made up of a variety of bonds that pays monthly income. As it turned out, the bond fund was essential in meeting her needs until the long-term care insurance was set to begin.

$MART CHOICES

Long-Term Care Insurance

- Insurance that covers at least part of the cost of nursing home care which is normally not covered by Medicare or regular health insurance

- May be used for in-home care

- Has a predetermined coverage period, three years to lifetime, depending on age when purchased

Bond Fund

- Mutual fund composed entirely of bonds: corporate, municipal, treasury, and any combination thereof

- Usually pays monthly income

- Can be taxable or tax-free

- Income can be reinvested in more shares

- Has no maturity date

- Share prices fluctuate in value—when interest rates rise, share prices go down

FRAN: THE SELF-DESCRIBED MEEK MOUSE

*"I don't want to get to the end of my life and find that I lived just
the length of it. I want to have lived the width of it as well."*

Diane Ackerman (1948 –)
American author

In every woman's life there is a moment of truth, where she
can either rise to the occasion or be a meek mouse. I admit that I have
lived most of my financial life as that meek mouse.

My first awareness of stocks came in the early fall of 1929,
when Bob, the young man I was dating, told me that he had bought
two shares of Cities Service stock and had persuaded his father to buy
ten shares. About a week or two later came the big crash. That intro-
duction to the world of high finance did not impress me.

After college graduation Bob and I were fortunate in getting
jobs, he in Detroit, I in New York. I made $170 a month for the ten
months of the school year. In the same block as my school building
there was a branch post office so it was more convenient for me to
open a postal savings account there than at a bank elsewhere. The
Bank Holiday of early 1933 did not affect my savings, and I was able
to send $100 postal money orders to my parents and to Bob so that
they could have pocket money. The following summer, Bob and I

were married. His salary was enough for living, and his bonus at Christmas allowed us to buy our first used car. We were launched.

As a salesman for Proctor and Gamble, Bob carried company money. Not wanting to confuse that money with our own, he turned over management of the family finances to me. I made out a big chart. Across the top I put all the headings: income, rent, food, clothing, recreation, and savings. Down the left side I put the dates for all our monthly expenses and recorded them every day. This was my first attempt at budgeting, and it at least helped me understand where we spent our money and showed me where I could save.

When Proctor and Gamble introduced Dreft detergent, the company offered a prize to the salesman who would best promote this revolutionary product. Bob won the prize, two shares of General Motors stock. I don't know how long we had it.

When we had been married three or four years, I received a legacy of $300 cash and some shares of United Fruit stock. The cash bought the lot my house was built on. I remember Bob saying that he would now be able to do some trading in stocks and my father telling him very definitely, "That is Fran's stock, not yours to play with! If she is able to have some things or some pleasure from it, no one outside the family will know you did not provide it yourself." My stock paid good dividends, and I held it for quite a few years, but I cannot remember using the dividends for any particular purpose. I did not reinvest. I eventually sold it so that we could participate with a sister and her husband in a real-estate purchase. I also inherited some interest in oil wells which paid oil royalties for a number of years.

Later, Bob went into business for himself and, although there were some bad times we weathered them. In fact, Bob did very well. He plowed profits back into his business and continually built it, while providing for our family very adequately, though not luxuriously.

I was forty-seven years old when our fourth and youngest child went to high school and no longer came home for the noon meal. I updated my skills and began working part-time at first, then full-time, at the occupation for which I had prepared in college, a medical technician. I qualified for Social Security and a small monthly pension check when I retired at age sixty-five. During those years Bob gradually closed his business and built up our portfolio at a major brokerage house.

I was never particularly interested in money. Bob was, so it was easy to leave the real responsibility to him. I remember him trying once or twice to tell me about our affairs. He would call me from whatever I was doing to stand beside him as he sat at his desk explaining. I did not say that I was getting tired standing there holding a dishtowel, or that this was an interruption, or that another time would be preferable. I just showed fatigue and lack of interest. After that happened two or three times, he gave up, saying that he guessed I would learn fast enough if I had to. At Bob's death in 1979, three-and-a-half years after my retirement, it all fell to me, and I had to learn. There was no more time to be the meek mouse.

Feeling lost and overwhelmed, I met with a financial adviser who suggested that I review my **asset allocation** and diversify investments into several categories. This, she assured me, would spread the risk between several investments and preserve income for my retirement. She also suggested a **balanced fund** of stocks and bonds to combine growth and more fixed investments. These recommendations proved to be a wise strategy and little by little my confidence in investing grew.

Since that time I've only had one full-fledged disaster. On the recommendation of my son's broker, I bought several shares of Portland General Corporation stock in 1988. All the income was reinvested from the start even after the company was converted into Enron. When Enron's investment scandal broke, I never received anything for the stock, and sold it for 1¢. That stinging loss caused me to be more cautious and see the true value of asset allocation and balanced investments.

My expenses increase each year I grow older and need to hire people to do more of the yard and housework I have always done for myself. The oil royalties have continued, with some fluctuations, for over fifty years, but I never know when production might end or something like an earthquake might destroy the wells. Without those monthly checks I would be dependent upon Social Security and the pension checks and whatever income there might be from investments.

Aware of my net worth and possible estate taxes, I sold some stocks and was able to gift each of my four children the $11,000 that may be given tax-free to an individual in a year.

My life is wonderful, and I have more than enough financial resources. I am grateful for my adviser who has educated me along the way and for my newfound ability to manage everything by myself. When the moment of truth came in my life, I did find my strength and now am the better for it.

ADVISER'S CORNER

*Fran is an intelligent, highly capable ninety-four-year-old widow. She lives in her own home, drives her car, and is very independent. She has owned a variety of stocks, bonds, and mutual funds, having done proper **asset allocation** based on her age, risk tolerance, and income needs. Her **balanced fund** initially consisted of 50% stocks and 50% bonds.*

As she's gotten older, I've put more of her investments into bonds and less into stocks, but she still maintains some growth instruments in her portfolio.

Fran comes in yearly with her son to review investments. She is able to live comfortably on her investment income, including oil royalties, without touching the principal. An ideal investor, she doesn't worry about market fluctuations and rarely makes changes in her portfolio.

 # $MART CHOICES

Asset Allocation

- The process of dividing investments into categories—usually cash, stocks, bonds, and real estate—based on the investor's age, risk tolerance, goals, and tax considerations

---

Balanced Fund

- Mutual fund invested in bonds, stocks, and cash

- Can be purchased in various classes of commission structure—front load or back end

- Managers of fund attempt to provide income, some growth, and preservation of capital

- Example: Franklin Income Fund
  - Pays monthly dividends
  - Current yield 6.5% (April 2004)
  - Can be reinvested

Part Three:
Advanced Strategies

MARIE: PLAYING HER OPTIONS

"One can never consent to creep when one feels an impulse to soar."

Helen Keller (1880 – 1968)
American blind and deaf educator

Last year I made an extra $120,000 on my portfolio by **selling naked puts**! I've always been a risk taker and this form of investing suits me, because I like my money in more aggressive instruments.

After our marriage, my husband William worked for a major corporation for close to twenty years, but we both knew that starting our own business was the fast lane to creating wealth. At first, he set up the business, and I did all of the office work including the bookkeeping. Then we decided to change the name of our company from a family name to a more generic name and I applied for the certification of Woman Owned Business and became CEO of the company. I did this in order to increase the scope of the business with the hopes of gaining more contracts.

Government contracts are supposed to be outsourced to a percentage of minorities and women. It was a good idea in theory, but in practice more contracts were awarded to minorities than to women. So we grew our business through networking new contacts, implementing quality control, marketing extensively, and gaining referrals from satisfied customers.

The business provides ample money to invest, and together we meet with a financial adviser who has put 100% of our money into growth stocks at our request. Bonds are boring. We want a more substantial return on our money. We feel our strategy has worked because we have nearly $850,000 in our portfolio.

As CEO of our company, I have sharpened my ability to research and analyze other companies. I subscribe to a monthly investment newsletter and get tips from its featured stock-picking expert. Then I go online and research these companies in depth for their growth potential. At that point, either I pick the stock, or my husband and I pick it together.

Our financial adviser taught me a strategy where I could sell naked puts for cash premiums and increase my portfolio by 10–15%. Last year these options were hardly ever exercised, and I was able to keep the cash premiums in my portfolio. Hence, the large gain.

In business and investing, my motto has always been "Seize the day!" Playing my options makes investing more fun and exciting!

ADVISER'S CORNER

Selling naked puts is an advanced strategy, more speculative than selling covered calls, and it works best in a flat market, where the seller will not be put (or exercised) to buy more stocks. But remember, past market performance is no indicator of future results, so any investor using this strategy should proceed with eyes wide open. Marie is a long-time stock investor who has traded stocks online, so this strategy was a match for both her skill level and her risk tolerance with more aggressive investments.

$MART CHOICE

Naked Put Option

- *Selling* (or writing) a *naked put* is a contract in which the seller of the put option is willing to buy a stock at a lower price by getting *put* or *exercised*

- Seller receives a *premium* or cash for selling a put. If at expiration the stock is above the strike price, the put option will expire

- Each put covers 100 shares of stock

- More speculative strategy than selling a covered call

- Example:
  - IBM stock price = $83.85 per share (July 2004)
  - Sell 10 puts (1,000 shares) for January 2005 @ $80 strike price (price at which she would be put or exercised to buy stock)
  - Premium received = $310 for each put option x 10 or $3,100 before commissions
  - If stock is below $80 on the third Friday of January 2005, investor will have to buy 1,000 shares of the stock at $80 per share
  - If stock is above $80, the *put* will expire
  - Investor will keep the $3,100 less commissions in either case

---

SUSAN: THE CHEERFUL GIVER

*"God loves a cheerful giver.
She gives best who gives with a smile."*

*Mother Teresa (1910 – 1997)
Albanian Catholic nun*

Some say that it is a woman's father who most shapes her relationship with the outside world. If that is true, then I had the best start a woman could wish for. My father believed in me and told me I could do anything I wanted with my life. When I was a child, that was learning the piano. When I was an adult, it was entering the male-dominated world of the brokerage business.

My father didn't try to direct me into one career over another. He just held this unfailing belief in my capabilities. He was a college professor, a brilliant man with master's degrees from Harvard and Yale and a doctorate. Even so, he earned a modest income of about $26,000 a year. On this modest salary he tithed 10% to the church and gave additional cash gifts to such charities as Goodwill and the Salvation Army. He was a man of strong faith and believed in the principles of Christian stewardship. My mother had been raised in a more affluent family and when they married, learned to live within my father's income, making many of our clothes and cutting expenses wherever she could.

From my father I learned the virtues of saving my money, giving generously from the heart, and investing in my own education. I began by obtaining a bachelor's degree at a local university. I worked two jobs when I was in school and every summer, so I didn't have to borrow money for my education. I then briefly worked in the medical industry before marrying and having my children. I wanted to be a stay-at-home mom when my children were younger.

I later finished my master's degree in education, taking classes one at a time around family commitments. While in graduate school, I met a woman in the investment industry who told me that it wasn't necessary to have a business degree to work in her field. She felt I had the people skills to make a great financial adviser.

To tell you the truth, I was surprised when a major brokerage house hired me into their training program. During the interview I had brazenly told them that I didn't care about money. I only cared about helping people, especially women. At the time I started, I had only a small personal account in a mutual fund, but by saving and following solid investment principles I was able to acquire some assets in my own right.

I was very successful in business because of my tenacity and my ability to network. The firm put me through a series of trainings and certifications in various financial investments, but it was truly my people skills that established my practice. I worked in partnership with a senior financial adviser who took me under his wing and mentored my skills along the way. Together, we pooled our strengths and built a strong base of clients and profitable business.

Years later, when my children were teenagers, I was facing the end of a twenty-three-year marriage. Tenacious till the end I tried everything to make it work but had to accept the fact that my husband did not want the marriage as much as I did. Because I was the major breadwinner, I was required to pay alimony to him. It was a very difficult time for me, as I had this obligation in addition to paying for my children's college education, cars, and other expenses.

Living through a divorce that challenged my lasting wealth made me all the more determined to rebuild and provide for my grown children. I was constantly on the lookout for strategies that would protect my post-divorce assets and allow me to leave as much money as possible to my children. My best investments had always been in real estate, and at the time I had three properties, one for each child and one I wanted to donate to charities.

I attended a seminar given by a hospital foundation and learned about setting up a **retained life estate**. This investment would allow me to donate a property, receive an immediate tax deduction which could be used over a six-year period, and still live in the property until my death.

I chose to donate a $130,000 condo that I owned debt-free. As the donor, I was still expected to pay all the expenses on the property: the taxes, insurance, and maintenance. Upon my death one-fourth of the proceeds from the sale of the condo will go to four charities: the children's hospital that introduced me to this investment, two Christian ministries of my choosing, and an organization that helps women in developing countries with small business loans. The foundation explained that I could change the beneficiaries of my gift at any time if I wanted different charities to benefit.

I also set up an **irrevocable life insurance trust** to pay off any estate taxes and one mortgage I had on another property. I am the insured, and this trust is both the owner and beneficiary of the life insurance. My attorney serves as the outside trustee.

Every year I pay my attorney the premium for the insurance, and she, by trust provisions, is obligated to write to my children and let them know that this premium is a gift to them, so they don't have to pay off any estate taxes or mortgage expenses. If my children were to ask for the cash equivalent of the premium, the insurance would not be in place, and they, not the trust, would be obligated to pay estate taxes and mortgage expenses upon my death. My children have always opted to pay the premium, but they are given this choice yearly and must sign off on the attorney's letter to maintain the insurance. This keeps my children in the loop and informed about the assets they will eventually inherit.

The day I donated the condo to the charities, I felt so happy because I had finally acknowledged all that God had given me. This legacy of charity is what I truly wish to leave my children, the same joy of giving my father bestowed on me.

ADVISER'S CORNER

People who have accumulated a net worth of $1 million or more have to be even more vigilant about protecting their money and assets for their heirs. In 2005 the current exemption from estate taxes is $1.5 million—all other assets and cash are taxed at a rate of 37–55%, depending on the individual's tax bracket. This exemption is scheduled to increase to $3.5 million by 2009, disappear in 2010, and then revert back to $1 million in 2011, unless Congress extends it. A financial adviser can help the investor re-evaluate suitability of investments for each life stage as well as recommend advanced estate planning strategies such as these to shelter assets. Planned giving is the perfect strategy for Susan for it is in sync with her personal and spiritual values and addresses her desire to leave the legacy of charity to her children.

$MART CHOICES

Retained Life Estate

- A planned-giving strategy in which the donor may gift a residence and continue to use it

- Donor receives an income-tax deduction for charitable contribution
  - May be used over six years, subject only to limitations in adjusted gross income

- Donor continues to pay all expenses on property: taxes, insurance, maintenance

- Donor can simplify estate planning and avoid estate tax on the value of the donated asset

- Perfect solution for couples or individuals whose children live in other areas and may have no use for this particular property

- Better to use this strategy with a debt-free property but can also be used if property has a mortgage

---

Irrevocable Life Insurance Trust (ILIT)

- Trust is the owner and beneficiary of the life insurance

- Individual is the insured

- Insured appoints an outside trustee to pay premiums and disburse trust proceeds upon death

- Death benefit is outside of the estate and protected from estate taxes, because it's owned by the trust

- Death benefit can be used by heirs to pay estate taxes on other assets or mortgages on other properties

- Life insurance policy can be *term* or *whole life* (*term:* insurance only for a certain time period such as 10, 15, or 20 years; *whole life:* insurance which builds a cash value and may be invested in a variety of mutual funds offered by the insurance company)

SARAH: BANKING ON HER HUSBAND

*"The effect of having other interests beyond those domestic works well.
The more one does and sees and feels, the more one is able to do,
and the more genuine may be one's appreciation of fundamental things
like home and love and understanding companionship."*

Amelia Earhart (1897 – 1937)
American aviator and author

When I was a young lady part of a woman's financial plan was to marry well, and I did just that. I married a bright, handsome man with great potential who lived only two blocks from me during my childhood years. I can't say that I had any true desire to be a career woman as my husband provided amply for me and our family.

My husband put together a major plan for a large city and was subsequently hired by a bank to work in the area of development. Throughout the years, he accumulated thousands of shares of stock in the bank with which he was affiliated. His cost for this stock was very low, and if we were to sell it, we would be faced with horrendous taxes on the capital gains.

My husband was very thorough with our financial planning and kept me informed about our money and assets. At one point we bought two Orange Julius franchises, and I served as the manager for these businesses. But I can honestly say that it was not a career I enjoyed, and the happiest day was the day we sold them.

When we got older, we decided that we really needed to focus on our estate planning so we could leave some assets for our children and grandchildren. We went to our estate-planning attorney to explore ways we could shelter these assets for our children and still donate some of our estate to charity. He suggested that we set up a **charitable remainder trust** and purchase a **second-to-die life insurance policy** to cover estate taxes and replace any income we donated to charity. We transferred our bank stock into the trust and donated a portion of our estate to a local charity. Then we purchased the second-to-die life insurance policy which insured us both with sufficient funds to cover estate taxes and restore our estate to its original amount for our heirs. Once we completed this estate planning, we had great peace of mind knowing that our life's wealth was protected.

Now women are cautioned not to depend on their husband's paycheck alone, to keep their hand in their career, even while raising children, and to save and invest for the future, all admirable recommendations for our time. It makes me appreciate even more, my precious, trustworthy husband and the freedom he gave me to be a stay-at-home mom and live life on my terms. Every woman deserves such a man in her corner. He was definitely my smartest choice.

ADVISER'S CORNER

Sarah was fortunate to have a successful husband who provided very well for his family. He worked for a bank for a long time and accumulated thousands of shares of that bank stock, which was the perfect gifting choice. They used this stock for the charitable remainder trust. This strategy works best for donors with substantial assets who wish to shelter holdings and make a gift to charity. Donors receive a current tax-deduction and monthly income based on the value of the assets transferred to the trust. This income goes to one or both donors until their death; then the assets go to the charity.

The second-to-die life insurance policy is the least expensive insurance one can buy, because the risk is spread between two people, and no death benefit is paid until the second person dies. It is primarily used to cover estate taxes and replace the asset amount donated to the charity.

$MART CHOICES

Charitable Remainder Trust (CRT)

- A planned-giving strategy in which assets in the trust are to be given to a tax-qualified charity such as a church, hospital, or nonprofit organization upon the donor's death

- Gives grantor a current tax deduction

- Income for life is based on the value of the assets placed in the trust which are re-valued annually

- Good for people who have highly-appreciated assets

(A) CRT Unitrust
- Can be funded with long-term appreciated assets to avoid capital-gains tax altogether
- Pays out an income stream based upon a minimum rate of 5%
- Income based upon value of trust assets which are re-valued annually
- Trust additions can be made at any time, resulting in new charitable deductions

(B) CRT Annuity Trust
- Can be funded with long-term appreciated assets to avoid capital-gains tax altogether
- Pays out income on a fixed rate based upon grantor's age and life expectancy (minimum 5%)
- Income fixed regardless of trust valuation
- May not add to trust principal

Second-to-Die Life Insurance Policy

- Least expensive life insurance one can buy

- Covers two people: spouses or business partners

- Doesn't pay death benefit until both people are deceased

- Death benefit is free from income tax

- Can be used to pay estate taxes

- Can be set up to replace amount of assets donated to charity, thus restoring estate to its original amount

---

ABIGAIL: THE TRIPLE-WIN SOLUTION

*"I personally measure success in terms of the contributions
an individual makes to her or his fellow human beings."*

Margaret Mead (1901 – 1978)
American anthropologist

As women we are often tested in life beyond what we think
we can physically and emotionally handle. My greatest test came the
year my husband died, and one of my grandchildren developed
leukemia. The grief was overwhelming, to lose the man I loved and
fear the loss of one so young at the same time.

I would not have made it through this trauma if it weren't for
the loving concern of those wonderful caregivers who worked at my
grandchild's hospital. They looked after me as much as they did my
grandchild.

When the illness had subsided, I wanted to give back to the
hospital to show them in some heartfelt way that I appreciated their
care at such a critical time. I spoke with my financial adviser, my
attorney, and members of the hospital foundation to design a mean-
ingful gift that was in sync with my estate planning. After exploring
all my options, I decided to set up a **charitable gift annuity**. This
allowed me to immediately make a gift to the hospital foundation and

receive an income-tax deduction the same year. Another advantage was that I would receive income for life from this arrangement. My team of advisers suggested that I buy a **flexible premium universal life insurance policy** with a death benefit of $100,000, the same amount I donated to the hospital.

This move turned out to be a triple-win solution: the hospital would benefit from my donation; I would receive both a tax deduction and monthly income, and my children would inherit an estate with the same valuation as that prior to my donation. It turned out to be the most gratifying investment I've ever made because it was so personal to me.

Staring death in the eye makes one sit up and notice what's truly important in life. In the end, it is only the love and compassion we extend to one another that matters and has any lasting value.

ADVISER'S CORNER

Abigail gave the foundation $100,000 from matured CDs which resulted in $600 monthly income until her death. She received a tax deduction of $41,652; however, since the deduction is limited to 50% of a person's adjusted gross income, her actual tax deduction will be $38,000, based upon her adjusted gross income (AGI) of $76,000. She can carry forward the remaining balance ($3,652) in her deduction into the next tax year.

Another distinct advantage of a charitable gift annuity is that Abigail need not declare all $7,200 of annual income as taxable. As a matter of fact, some 68.7% of the income will be tax-free every year up to her life expectancy, which is about 11.8 years at age seventy-six (based on actuarial tables). If she outlives her life expectancy, the entire annual income amount becomes taxable as ordinary income.

Abigail will receive a $41,652 tax deduction for the charitable gift annuity. This will partially purchase a life insurance policy with a one-time premium payment of $44,411 and a death benefit of $100,000 to replace the gift to charity.

The detailed example on the following page shows how this charitable gift provided more income than transferring the same $100,000 into another CD rollover:

Comparison between a **CD Rollover** and a **Charitable Gift Annuity** for Abigail, widow, age seventy-six (AGI = Adjusted Gross Income)

<u>CD Rollover</u>

AGI $76,768
$100,000 @ 3% for 5 years

<u>3%</u>	
$3,000	
<u>25%</u>	income tax bracket
$750	taxes owed
$2,250	**net income per year**

No tax deduction

<u>Charitable Gift Annuity</u>

AGI $76,000
$100,000 @ 7.2% for life

<u>7.2%</u>	
$7200	68.7% tax free for a life expectancy which is 11.8 years
$2232	31.3% taxable
<u>25%</u>	income tax bracket
$558	taxes owed
$6,575	**net income per year**

$MART CHOICES

Charitable Gift Annuity

- A planned gift funded with cash or appreciated assets

- Generates an income tax deduction for charitable contributions in same year gift made

- High level of income received

- Usually partially tax-free

- Reduces federal estate tax if applicable

- Enables donor to enjoy satisfaction of charitable giving

Flexible Premium Universal Life Insurance

- Also known as *universal life insurance,* a whole life insurance policy that builds cash value

- Individual is insured

- Monthly administrative policy charges apply

- Monthly interest credited

- Flexibility in premium level and frequency of payment

- Policy withdrawals and loans available

JANI: ART AND ARCHITECTURE

*"It is good do have an end to journey toward,
but it is the journey that matters in the end."*

Ursula K. LeGuin (1929 –)
American author

One of my earliest childhood memories is traveling up the long, winding driveway to my grandparents' mansion, an elegant home with antiques, oriental rugs, and servants who greeted us at the door. Grandpa was a builder of these mansions, and I was fascinated with all the beauty and detail of the architecture. Because of this early influence, I have always been attracted to real estate as an investment.

As a girl and young woman, I never thought of my houses as investments but rather creative projects, homes I could fix up and decorate. I have since bought and sold ten to twelve houses in my lifetime which constitutes the majority of my net worth. I purchased my first home in the '70s for $14,000 and sold it a year-and-a-half later for $19,000. I then took that profit and invested it in my next home.

I've always had a strong intuitive sense about which houses to buy. I knew immediately if the house was the right fit for me, and I never changed my mind about owning it. I looked for houses with good bones, a solid floor plan that needed little changing and facilitated an ease of living and flow. Then my artist mind went to work as I imagined how to shape and fill the space. Many of the changes I made were cosmetic—paint, tile, carpet—but sometimes I would remove a wall or two to create open space or showcase a view to the mountains. That's when I felt Grandpa's eye for design come through.

Now that I'm in my 60s, I currently own five properties—my beach home, a condo in a nearby city, a resort property in Arizona, and my newest purchases, a rental property in New York and a condo in California. When I bought my resort property in Arizona, it was my third property in the same area which is blessed with sunshine and year-round great weather. I purchased it as my winter residence to escape the cold winters in the Midwest and especially liked the single-story floor plan as I was thinking about my old age and that of my husband who is ten years my senior.

The home was over thirty years old and need many improvements. I spent hours imagining how I could make this my personal oasis. I never dreamed it would appreciate $400,000 in the last four years. It has also become a profitable rental property. While I summered back in my beach house, I rented my Arizona home for $12,000 for a few months, which paid for all the taxes, utilities, maintenance, and the gardener. I had purchased this property with cash, so there were no mortgage payments.

I have enjoyed this resort home but felt it was more house than I needed. I wanted to downsize to a smaller, more manageable place. Some friends told me about a small one-bedroom condo for sale right down the street, and I thought this would be just the property to own. It would still be a great summer rental and accommodate me nicely for the winters. I bought it immediately before I listed my current property and was shocked later when my C.P.A. told me that I would owe $135,000 in capital gains taxes from the sale of my house. That's when I investigated a **1031 tax-deferred exchange**. The IRS allows people to defer paying capital gains taxes if they exchange properties for an equal or greater value.

Because I purchased my condo before I sold my current home, which is considered the *relinquished property*, I'm doing what's called a **reverse exchange**; and this requires the services of an *accommodator* or qualified intermediary who will take title to the property and hold everything until the exchange closes. This costs approximately $5,000–$10,000.

I have also chosen to have them do the improvements on my condo, which will be added to my cost basis on that property. I will fax them the list of improvements I'm doing in the remodel, and they will sign off on the construction costs and pay the contractors from my escrow proceeds. This is called an **improvements exchange**

I purchased the new condo for $345,000 and will do $30,000 of improvements which will total $375,000. My current home will sell for $895,000, which will net $855,000 after real estate commissions and other expenses. Therefore, I must purchase another property which, combined with the condo, will equal or exceed my net proceeds of $855,000. I have targeted another rental property in New York which will satisfy that requirement. Therefore, I will pay no tax on my gain. Since this property will be purchased after the sale of my home, it is considered a **delayed exchange**. According to the rules of exchange, this property had to be targeted within forty-five days after closing the sale of the relinquished property and must close within 180 days of the same date, so timing is of the essence.

To be honest, the timing has been the most stressful part of these exchanges, but when I am done, I will have saved $135,000 in taxes and own two new beautiful properties. It's sort of like playing Monopoly—I get to pick and choose several properties on the board and exchange them tax-free! And, even though I won't be rushing out to do another triple exchange in the near future, I'm thrilled to have mastered this strategy for future use.

ADVISER'S CORNER::

The 1031 tax exchange is a tax-deferral strategy that can be used for business or investment properties only, not for primary residences. This advanced strategy is not for novice investors, but those who can juggle multiple transactions and the challenges that come with them

Jani's current net worth is in excess of $2 million because she has acted upon her intuitive sense of properties. It has been her major wealth-building strategy. The 1031 tax exchange allows her to keep her money in play in other equity-building properties.

$MART CHOICE

1031 Tax-Deferred Exchange

- IRS tax-deferral strategy which allows property owner to exchange equity in property and defer capital gains tax, provided replacement property is equal to or greater in value than net proceeds from existing (relinquishing) property

- Property owner is considered the *exchanger*

- *Accommodator* is a qualified intermediary who takes title of replacement property and executes all escrow instructions for exchange

- Services of accommodator needed for reverse, improvement, and delayed exchanges

- *Reverse exchange* occurs when replacement property is purchased before the sale of the relinquishing property

- *Delayed exchange* occurs when the replacement property is purchased after the sale of the relinquishing property

- *Improvements exchange* occurs when accommodator monitors improvements on replacement property and pays contractors from escrow proceeds (added to cost basis of property)

Part Four:
The Starter Guide
to $mart Choices

ACTION STEPS

1. Fill out the Personal Financial Profile.

2. Choose a financial adviser.

3. Review your assets, goals, and objectives with your financial adviser.

4. Implement the strategies selected with regard to asset allocation and specific investments.

5. Track your investments monthly.

6. Have a semiannual review of investments with your adviser.

7. Organize your whole life in one notebook.

8. Consider joining an investment club and NAIC for ongoing practice researching companies and picking your investments.

9. Learn all you can about your money and investments. (See Recommended Reading.)

10. Enjoy your money and count your blessings.

PERSONAL FINANCIAL PROFILE

A good profile questionnaire will include the following:

✔ **FAMILY CENSUS DATA:** all family members' names, birthdates, social security numbers

✔ **EMPLOYMENT DATA:** income, tax bracket, expected retirement dates

✔ **CONTACT INFORMATION:** address, phone and fax numbers, email addresses

✔ **ALL ASSETS:** (and how they are titled)

- Real Estate: value, purchase price and date, rental income, how titled (joint, single, trust)

- Cash and Cash Equivalents: where, interest rate, how titled

- Annuities: purchase amount, type (fixed or variable) yield, how titled, beneficiary, death benefit

- Bonds: tax free or taxable, yield, purchase price and date, maturity date, current value, how titled

- Bond Funds: open end or closed end, class A, B, C or other, purchase price and date, how titled

- Unit Trusts: purchase price and date, how titled

- Certificates of Deposit: bank, purchase price and date, maturity date, yield, how titled

- Common Stocks: name of company, number of shares, current value, purchase price and date, how titled

- Balanced Funds: purchase price and date, current value, how titled

- Retirement Plans: type, institutions, purchase price and date, current value, current yield, beneficiaries

- Life Insurance: Insured, company, premiums, value, death benefit, owner, beneficiary

- Disability Insurance: company, premium, benefit, waiting period

- Long-term Care Insurance: company, premium, waiting period, length of policy

✔ **LIABILITIES:** All debts

✔ **NET WORTH:** All assets minus all liabilities

✔ **ESTATE PLANNING:** Wills, trusts

✔ **BUSINESS OWNERSHIP:** Cash, real estate, equipment

HOW TO ORGANIZE YOUR WHOLE LIFE IN ONE NOTEBOOK

1. Buy a three-ring four inch binder.

2. Organize categories alphabetically:

   • Example: Automobile Titles, Bank Statements, Certificates of Deposit, Life Insurance Policies, Living Trust, etc.

   • Customize for unique categories such as Fur Storage or Certificates of Authenticity for art and collectibles.

3. Place all important documents in plastic sheet protectors.

4. Replace statements monthly with new statements.

5. Save all tax returns and supporting data for seven years.

6. Save only year-end retirement plan statements.

7. Incorporate all estate planning documents including living trust.

8. Write funeral wishes.

9. Notify family members and trustees of location of this book.

10. Store in a safe place.

GUIDELINES FOR CHOOSING YOUR FINANCIAL ADVISER

Interview and select a financial adviser who:

- Has many years of experience

- Works for a good, financially healthy company

- Listens to you and does a complete financial profile

- Makes recommendations on a total financial plan with no regard to commissions he or she will earn

- Makes appropriate asset-allocation suggestions based on your age, risk tolerance and objectives (asset categories are real estate, stocks, bonds, and cash)

- Makes appropriate estate planning recommendations in conjunction with a good estate planning attorney

- Works well with your C.P.A.

- Provides frequent reviews of your accounts and objectives

In other words, choose someone who really cares about **YOU** and will take the time to educate you about your investments.

RECOMMENDED READING AND RESOURCES

BOOKS

Bach, David. Start Late, Finish Rich. New York: Broadway Books, 2005.

Bach, David. The Automatic Millionaire. New York: Broadway Books, 2003.

Bach, David. The Automatic Millionaire Workbook. New York: Broadway Books, 2005.

Bach, David. Smart Women Finish Rich. New York: Broadway Books, 2002.

Bach, David. Smart Couples Finish Rich. New York: Broadway Books, 2002.

Bach, David. The Finish Rich Workbook. New York: Broadway Books, 2003.

Bahr, Candace, and Ginita Wall. It's More Than Money—It's Your Life. Indianapolis: Wiley and Sons, 2004.

Blue, Ron. Taming the Money Monster. Wheaton: Tyndale, 1999.

Blue, Ron, and Judy Blue. A Woman's Guide to Financial Peace of Mind. Colorado Springs: Focus on the Family, 1991.

Blue, Ron. Sneakers. Insight for Living, 1991. (out of print)

Blue, Ron, and Judy Blue. Raising Money Smart Kids. Nashville: Thomas Nelson, 1992.

Blue, Ron. Master Your Money Workbook. Nashville: Thomas Nelson, 1993.

Blue, Ron. Storm Shelter. Nashville: Thomas Nelson, 1994.

Blue, Ron. Generous Living. Grand Rapids: Zondervan, 1997.

Blue, Ron, and Judy Blue. Money Talks and So Can We. Grand Rapids: Zondervan, 1999.

Blue, Ron, and Larry Burkett. Wealth to Last. Broadman Holman Publishing, 2003.

Blue, Ron. Splitting Heirs. Chicago: Moody Press, 2004.

Blue, Ron. The New Master Your Money. Chicago: Moody Press, 2004.

Burkett, Larry. How to Manage Your Money: An In-depth Bible Study on Personal Finances. Chicago: Moody Press, 2002.

Durling, Sharon. A Girl and Her Money: How to Have a Great Relationship Without Falling in Love. Nashville: W. Publishing Group, 2003.

Glink, Ilyce R. 50 Simple Things You Can Do to Improve Your Personal Finances: How to Spend Less, Save More, and Make the Most of What You Have. New York: Three Rivers Press, 2001.

Godfrey, Joline. 20 Secrets to Money Independence: The Dollar Diva's Guide to Life. New York: St. Martin's Press, 2000.

Hunt, Mary. Debt-proof Your Marriage: How to Achieve Financial Harmony. New York: Fleming H. Revell, 2003.

Kennedy, Diane. Loopholes of the Rich: How the Rich Legally Make More Money and Pay Less Tax. New York: Warner Books, 2001.

Kiyosaki, Robert, and Sharon Lechter. Rich Dad! Success Stories.

New York: Warner Books, 2003.

Kobliner, Beth. Get a Financial Life: Personal Finance in Your Twenties and Thirties. New York: Simon & Schuster, 2000.

Mellan, Olivia, and Sherry Christie. Money Shy to Money Sure: A Woman's Roadmap to Financial Well Being. New York: Walker, 2001.

Orman, Suze. Suze Orman's Protection Portfolio: Will and Trust Kit. Carlsbad: Hay House, 2002. (Read all of Suze Orman's books.)

Perry, Ann. The Wise Inheritor: How to Protect It, Grow It and Enjoy It. New York: Broadway Books, 2003.

Quinn, Jane Bryant. Making the Most of Your Money. New York: Simon & Schuster, 1997.

Ragolia, Stacia. The Frugal Woman's Guide to a Rich Life. Nashville: Thomas Nelson, 2003.

Ramsey, David. Financial Peace. Nashville: Thomas Nelson, 2003.

Ramsey, David. The Total Money Makeover. Nashville: Thomas Nelson, 2003.

Ramsey, David. The Total Money Makeover Workbook. Nashville: Thomas Nelson, 2003.

Resnick, Judy. I've Been Rich. I've Been Poor. Rich is Better: How Every Woman Can Find Economic Security and Personal Freedom. New York: St. Martin's Press, 1998.

Shelton, Phyllis. R. Long-term Care: Your Financial Planning Guide. New York: Kensington Publishing, 2003.

Stanley, Thomas, and William Danko. The Millionaire Next Door. Marietta: Longstreet Press, 1996.

Stav, Julie. Fund Your Future: Winning Strategies for Managing Your Mutual Funds and 405(k). New York: Berkley Publishing, 2001.

Twist, Lynne. The Soul of Money: Transforming Your Relationship With Money and Life. New York: W.W. Norton, 2003.

Women Count: Smart About Money. [Videotape] Greenwich, CT.: Third Wave Television.

WEB SITES

MindGrind, [No date], "The Money Club," [Online], http://www.moneyclubs.com, [September 19, 2004].

MindGrind, [No date], "WIFE.org, Women's Institute for Financial Education," [Online], http://www.wife.org, [September 19, 2004].

Lightbulb Press, [No date], "Lightbulb Online Dictionary of Financial Terms," [Online], http://www.lightbulbpress.com/onlinedictionary/onlinedictionary.html, [September 19, 2004].

www.davidbach.com

www.davidramsey.com

www.savingforcollege.com

www.yahoofinance.com

GLOSSARY

Annuities—
Annuities are investment contracts with insurance companies. The earnings and growth are tax-deferred until withdrawn. The insurance company guarantees a certain rate of return or minimum interest rate. There are surrender charges for most annuities as well as annual fees and expenses.

Asset Allocation—
Asset allocation is the process of dividing investments into categories—usually cash, stocks, bonds, and real estate—based on the investor's age, risk tolerance, goals, and tax considerations. The investor may also have sub-asset categories such as growth and international stocks.

Balanced Fund—
A *balanced fund* is a mutual fund that invests typically in bonds, stocks, and cash. The managers of the fund attempt to provide income, some growth, and preservation of capital. Typically the price will be more stable than a stock fund.

Basis (Cost Basis)—
The *cost basis* is the price paid for an asset or an adjusted price due to external factors. When the stock portfolio or real property is inherited, the cost basis becomes the price at the date of death. When real property is improved, the cost basis is adjusted to include capital improvements.

Blue-chip Stocks—
Blue-chip stocks are stocks in big, recognized companies such as Microsoft, that have large cash positions (liquidity) and great earnings.

Bonds—
A *bond* is a loan to a company, municipality, or government. The

bond holder is paid interest, usually semi-annually. Each bond has a fixed rate of interest and a maturity date. They are rated from AAA (the highest grade) down to junk (C and below).

Bond Funds—

A *bond fund* is a mutual fund composed entirely of bonds: corporate, municipal, treasury, and any combination thereof. The fund usually pays a monthly income which can change based on economic conditions. This monthly income can be reinvested in more shares of the fund, and the fund has no maturity date.

Certificates of Deposit (CD's)—

Certificates of deposit are investments issued by banks, with a fixed rate of interest and definite maturity dates. They may also be offered by brokerage houses and function like bonds. They are insured by FDIC (Federal Deposit Insurance Corporation) up to $100,000 and are considered very safe investments.

Charitable Remainder Trust—

A *charitable remainder trust* is a trust set up for the purpose of gifting to a tax-qualified charity. The investor receives an income tax deduction and income based on the value of the assets given. The assets, once in the trust, can be sold income tax-free. At death, the principal is paid to the charity.

Closed-end Fund—

A *closed-end fund* is a mutual fund that is closed after a set number of shares have been sold to the public. The investor can buy or sell shares on an exchange, and the shares are traded just like stock.

College Savings Plans—

College savings plans are specific accounts offered by banks and brokerage houses to make tax-free gifting to children easier. Examples are the Uniform Gift to Minors Act (UGMA), Uniform Transfers to Minors Act (UTMA), Coverdell Education Savings Accounts, and 529 Plans.

Common Stock—
Common stock represents shares in a company that are publicly traded on exchanges such as the New York Stock Exchange (NYSE) or American Stock Exchange (AMEX).

Dividends—
Dividends are cash payments paid to shareholders, usually paid quarterly.

Expiration Date—
Expiration date is a term used in options buying and selling. All options expire on the third Friday of the month.

Estate Taxes—
Estate taxes are the taxes due on the net values of an estate (life insurance, real property, investments) after death. There is an exception for married couples who have an unlimited marital deduction if one spouse dies before the other.

401K Plan—
A *401K Plan* is a voluntary retirement plan offered within a corporation or company, to which employees may contribute a percentage of their pre-tax earnings. The employer often offers a match, and many investment choices are available.

403B Plan—
A *403B Plan* is a similar retirement savings plan to the 401K, offered to employees of non-profit organizations.

Front-end Load—
A *front-end load* is an up-front fee or commission to purchase shares in a mutual fund, payable to the broker at the time of purchase. These shares are referred to as Class A shares.

Gifting: Uniform Gifts/Transfers to Minors Act (UGMA/UTMA)—
UGMA and *UTMA* accounts are custodial accounts opened in a child's name and social security number and transfer to the child at age 18 or 21, depending on the state of residence. Cash placed

in these accounts may be used to purchase many different investments.

Growth Funds—

Growth funds are mutual funds that invest in the stocks of companies that are likely to grow in value and increase earnings. These are suitable for long-term investments.

Growth Stocks—

Growth stocks are stocks whose primary objective is to grow share price rather than pay out dividends to shareholders. The increased net profits of the company are usually reflected in higher share prices over time.

Home Equity Loans—

A *home equity loan* is a loan secured by the equity ownership in the home. The homeowner can usually borrow up to 80% of the value (loan to value) of the home minus the mortgage debt. Qualification depends on income and debt-to-equity ratios. There are usually no costs or very low costs to obtain these loans.

Income Fund—

An *income fund* is a mutual fund usually invested in bonds and high yield stocks. Most pay monthly dividends/interest and are more stable in price than stock funds.

IRA (Individual Retirement Account)

An *IRA* is an individual retirement account in which the investor may deduct the contribution from pre-tax income and reduce taxes.

*Rollover—

The *rollover* allows the investor to transfer assets from a qualified plan such as a 401K or 403B into an individual IRA and pay no tax at the time.

*Roth IRA—

The *Roth IRA* allows the investor to deposit after-tax money and pay no tax when the money is withdrawn within specified guide-lines.

*SEP IRA—

SEP stands for *Simplified Employee Pension* IRA in which a self-employed individual may contribute a larger percentage of her earnings to retirement than in a traditional or Roth IRA.

Laddering—

Laddering is an excellent way to structure a bond portfolio, where the bonds mature or come due at staggered dates to meet income and capital needs and to protect against interest rate risk.

Life Insurance

A life insurance policy can be *term* or *whole life* (*term*: insurance only for a certain time period such as 10, 15, 20 years; *whole life*: insurance which builds a cash value and may be invested in a variety of mutual funds offered by the insurance company.

Life Insurance Trust

A *life insurance trust* protects life insurance proceeds from estate taxes, because the trust is the policy holder and the death benefit does not get added into the total value of the estate.

Living Trust—

A *living trust* is a revocable, changeable written agreement to des-ignate who will manage the *trustor's* (grantor of the trust) assets during life, incapacity, and death. The assets must be funded or re-titled in the name of the trust to be protected by the trust—for example, real estate must be re-titled in the name of the trust with a quit-claim deed.

The trustor names a *trustee* or trustees to administer the trust in the trustor's incapacity or death. When properly executed the trust includes a *will* and *a durable power of attorney for health care.*

Municipal Bond—

A *municipal bond* is a bond that is issued by a city, county, or state government and pays tax-free interest.

Mutual Fund—
A *mutual fund* is an investment in the stocks or bonds of several companies, which spreads the risk of ownership among these companies versus the higher risk of ownership in individual stocks or bonds.

Option—
An *option* is the right, but not the obligation, to buy or sell stock at a specified price on or before a specific date.

P/E Ratio—
The *P/E ratio* is the *price* of the stock divided by the *earnings* per share. Stocks with lower P/E ratios, have more value and are generally considered to be less risky investments.

Preferred Stock—
A *preferred stock* is a class of stock that, like a bond, pays a fixed dividend, usually distributed quarterly.

Premium—
A *premium* is:
a. the price paid for insurance policies or
b. the cash received or paid in buying or selling an option contract.

Probate—
Probate is the process of settling an estate according to the wishes of an individual in a written document called a will. This process can be lengthy and costly, and can be avoided by having a properly funded living trust.

Prenuptial Agreement—
A *prenuptial agreement* is a contract drawn prior to marriage which specifies how assets would be divided in the case of a divorce. This agreement is often used in a second marriage to protect assets for the individuals and their families.

529 Savings Plan—

A *529 Savings Plan* is a tax-deferred college savings plan run by states and set up with mutual fund companies. The money may be used to pay higher education expenses at any accredited college or university in the country.

Second-to-Die Life Insurance—

A *second-to-die life insurance policy* is the least expensive life insurance one can buy. It covers two people, usually spouses or business partners, and doesn't pay a death benefit until both people are deceased.

Stock—

A *stock* is partial ownership in a company in exchange for money. Stocks are bought and sold in shares.

Treasury Bond—

A *treasury bond* is a bond issued by the U.S. Government that has the highest quality rating of AAA. The interest earned on the bond is taxable at the federal level, but not at the state or local level.

Value Stocks—

Value stocks are stocks that represent a good buy relative to the company's assets—that is, they are undervalued in price with an excellent potential for profit.

Yield to Maturity (YTM)—

The *yield to maturity* is the actual yield of a bond (or return on investment) to the maturity value of the bond, depending on the coupon and price of the bond.

Zero Coupon Bonds—

Zero coupon bonds are bonds which pay no current interest but appreciate in value by a specific maturity date. These can be offered by cities, corporations, and county or state governments.